C0 6GC 682

Recollecting the Arundel Circle

Literature and the Visual Arts
New Foundations

Ernest B. Gilman
General Editor

Vol. 16

PETER LANG
New York • Washington, D.C./Baltimore • Bern
Frankfurt am Main • Berlin • Brussels • Vienna • Oxford

Ernest B. Gilman

Recollecting the Arundel Circle

Discovering the Past, Recovering the Future

PETER LANG
New York • Washington, D.C./Baltimore • Bern
Frankfurt am Main • Berlin • Brussels • Vienna • Oxford

Library of Congress Cataloging-in-Publication Data

Gilman, Ernest B.
Recollecting the Arundel Circle: discovering the past,
recovering the future / Ernest B. Gilman.
p. cm. — (Literature and the visual arts; vol. 16)
Includes bibliographical references (p.) and index.
1. Arundel, Thomas Howard, Earl of, 1585–1646—Art patronage.
2. Arundel, Thomas Howard, Earl of, 1585–1646—Friends and associates.
3. Art patronage—Great Britain—History—17th century. 4. Great
Britain—Intellectual life—17th century. I. Title. II. Series.
N5247.A78 G55 709'.2—dc21 2002006256
ISBN 0-8204-6147-4
ISSN 0888-3890

Die Deutsche Bibliothek-CIP-Einheitsaufnahme

Gilman, Ernest B.:
Recollecting the Arundel circle: discovering the past,
recovering the future / Ernest B. Gilman.
–New York; Washington, D.C./Baltimore; Bern;
Frankfurt am Main; Berlin; Brussels; Vienna; Oxford: Lang.
(Literature and the visual arts; Vol. 16)
ISBN 0-8204-6147-4

Cover art: Anthony Van Dyck, *Thomas Howard, Earl of Arundel, and the Countess of Arundel* (The "Madagascar" Portrait), 1639. Oil on canvas (139.7 × 212.7 cm). Version (possibly a copy "after" Van Dyck) at Knole, Sevenoaks, Kent. Private Collection. Photo: Photographic Survey, Coutauld Institute of Art, London.

The paper in this book meets the guidelines for permanence and durability
of the Committee on Production Guidelines for Book Longevity
of the Council of Library Resources.

© 2002 Peter Lang Publishing, Inc., New York

All rights reserved.
Reprint or reproduction, even partially, in all forms such as microfilm,
xerography, microfiche, microcard, and offset strictly prohibited.

Printed in the United States of America

For Seth and Eve

Figli Carissimi

Table of Contents

Illustrations

Acknowledgments

Over the last several years, parts of this study have been published in earlier versions: Chapter 1 in *Early Modern Visual Culture: Representation, Race, and Empire in Renaissance England*, ed. Peter Erickson and Clark Hulse, University of Pennsylvania Press (2000), and Chapter 2 in *Opening the Borders: Inclusivity and Early Modern Literature, Essays in Honor of James V. Mirollo*, ed. Peter G. Herman, University of Delaware Press/ Associated University Press (1999). I am grateful to the editors of these collections for their careful reading of my work; to those institutions listed with the illustrations, for permission to use the images of paintings by Van Dyck and Daniel Mytens in their possession; to the trustees of Arundel Castle and Knole for their hospitality during my research; and to the Abraham and Rebecca Stein Faculty Publications Fund of New York University and the Solomon R. Guggenheim Foundation for their support of this project. The following have, at one time or another, offered their expertise, kindness and encouragement along the road to this book: Christopher Brown, Martin Elsky, Phillip Fehl, Rosanna Giammarino, Louise Govier, James Heffernan, Tara Hoag, Jack Irwin, and W.J.T. Mitchell. It is my pleasure to achknowledge the friendship and support of my colleagues at New York University, especially Mary Carruthers, Una Chaudhuri, Roger Deakins, John Freccero, Dustin Griffin, David Hoover, Daniel Javitch, Anthony Low, Michael Rampino, Jeffrey Spear, Gabrielle Starr, and Deborah Winiarski. This book is dedicated, with all a father's love, to my children, Eve and Seth Gilman, and to their mother.

Introduction: The "Collector" Earl and his Circle

This book traces the network of connections among a small group of writers and painters, diverse in their interests and distinguished in their individual accomplishments, all of them surrounding Thomas Howard, 14th Earl of Arundel, in the 1630s. Its focus is on understanding the relationship between two ventures that preoccupied Arundel and came, more or less directly, to involve those around him: the Earl's lifelong passion for the collection of antiquities, and his momentary enthusiasm for founding a colony on the island of Madagascar in 1639. Arundel is a fascinating contradiction, in his way like Thomas More—a man in the world but not of it, introspective, reticent, but destined to play a highly visible role on the artistic and intellectual stage of Stuart England. Cultural histories recall him as one of the three great art collectors of the period, rivaled in the 1620s by James's favorite, the mercurial George Villiers, Duke of Buckingham, and then after the succession of the new King, by Charles I himself. With the assassination of Buckingham in 1628, Arundel divided the field only with the King. Even in such company, Arundel's role as a collector was arguably the more significant.

The King's most spectacular acquisitions—the Banqueting House ceiling commissioned from Rubens at a fee of £3000, and the cabinet of the Duke of Mantua purchased for £18,000 (in borrowed money)—were the exceptions to a more frugal rule on such expenditures, one enforced by the chronically imperiled condition of the royal Exchequer (see Smuts, "Political Failure" 174–76). In contrast, Arundel's efforts over a thirty-year period reflect a singular dedication that enabled the Earl to extend his influence and the scope of his collections from Italy to Greece and the Levant, making his presence felt in an international arena once reserved for Medici princes and Hapsburg emperors. Although nearly all his pictures were dispersed after his death in 1646, the Arundel Marbles would remain as his monument. The history of connoisseurship in England would claim him as its patron saint, the model of the learned and discerning collector. To Horace Walpole in the eighteenth century, Arundel was the "father of virtú in England." At Arundel Castle in Sussex, he is still distinguished from his forebears and his successors as the "Collector" Earl.

What has been given only passing attention in this account is that, more ardently than his competitors, Arundel was also a collector of brilliant men who stood within the circle of his patronage. His relation to them was closer than that of other English patrons to their cultural clients. Within a patronage system, artists might hope for occasional commissions, poets for gifts of money in return for fawning dedications, or at best for a sinecure in the patron's household—if not, through the patron's influence, at court. One place open to men of letters was that of tutor to the patron's children, the position held in Arundel House by Franciscus Junius, the Earl's librarian. A man of Junius's antiquarian and philological talents might also have prudent advice to offer from time to time on contemporary matters since (as Sidney has his historian boast) he speaks as *magistra vitae* and *nuntia vetustatis*.

As a hapless petitioner might discover, however, the system of aristocratic patronage depends as much, if not more, on the patron's distance from the client—on his power to disdain and refuse—as on any bond of sympathy. The collapse of Donne's hopes of secular preferment after his marriage dramatized the exercise of that power in a particularly brutal way. But Donne's undoing was far from unique, since an anxiety about the precariousness of the patron's favor was the inescapable malaise of the hopeful. Arundel appears to have been the exception. He had an eye out for scholars like Junius and artists like Van Dyck or the engraver Wenceslas Hollar who might be attracted into his own service or recommended to the court. The ties he forged were enduring and were characterized by mutual respect In the case of Junius and his contemporaries in Arundel's employ, the work they undertook embodied the Earl's ambitions just as much as his encouragement and resources facilitated their own ends. As neither can be understood without the other, the object of study in what follows is not primarily Arundel himself or the several projects of those in his service, but rather the cultural field defined by their collaboration.

As the premier Earl of the kingdom and the possessor of a substantial fortune through his marriage in 1606 to Aletheia Talbot, granddaughter of Bess of Hardwick, Arundel in his twenties had cut a prominent figure at James's court. He took part in Ben Jonson's *Hymenaei* and other entertainments. In 1609 Aletheia appeared as Atalanta in Jonson's *Masque of Queens* (an Inigo Jones drawing of her costume survives). Over the winter of 1612–1613, the couple also attended the prolonged festivities surrounding the engagement and marriage of the Princess Elizabeth to the Elector Palatine—including, we must suppose, the production of *The Tempest* staged at court as part of those nuptial celebrations. At the wedding ceremony itself "the Earl of Arundel carried the Sword, walking immediately before the King" (Hervey 70). Afterwards, Arundel and the Countess escorted the newlyweds on their voyage down the Rhine to their new home in the Palatinate. Yet despite his prominence at court in times of good fortune and ill, and notwithstanding his considerable skill in the dicey pursuit of titles and preferment, Arundel always took pains to set himself off from his flashier rivals.

Arundel's boyhood, like Donne's, was darkened by the tragedies of Elizabethan religious conflict. His Catholic grandfather had been executed as a traitor for his loyalty to the old religion. While his father Philip languished in the Tower on suspicion of the same charge, Arundel's mother offered the shelter of their home in the north to clandestine Jesuit priests, including the recusant poet Robert Southwell. In 1595, when Arundel was ten, his father—whose imprisonment had begun before the birth of his son—finally evaded the daily possibility of a death warrant from the Queen by dying in his cell. Arundel would surely have heard of Southwell's more gruesome fate in the same year, when the priest was hanged, disemboweled, and beheaded. Shadowed by such memories, Arundel, in his early twenties, seemed naturally to gravitate from the splendor of court life toward the graver company surrounding Prince Henry, until the untimely death of the young heir to the throne in 1612. Every portrait we have of Arundel shows a withdrawn aspect, meditative and melancholy. Graham Parry offers a deft character sketch of the Earl:

> Arundel's temperament was haughty and austere; his secluded upbringing and the consciousness of his high ancestry promoted a certain aloofness which intensified as he grew older. He had few close friends, and sought intellectual companionship rather than social conviviality. He was a man of integrity in a reign not noted for high principles at Court; he was statesman rather than a politician, an aristocrat rather than a courtier. Even his dress marked his distance from his peers, for he is shown in all his portraits in sober and subdued clothes, or in plain armour,looking more like a Venetian senator than a Jacobean courtier. (109)

However reserved his demeanor, Arundel was ardent to the point of extravagance in his artistic pursuits. His eyes were opened to Italian art during an extended journey on the continent in 1613–14 in the company of Inigo Jones. From then until the final reversal of his fortunes at the time of the Civil War, Arundel lavished enormous sums on his collections. The Jacobean fashion for pictures and "antiquities," largely set by Arundel himself, was aped on a smaller scale by men of lesser discernment and fewer means. It was the Earl, however, who came to exemplify the distinction between the mere accumulator of valuable works of art and the connoisseur. Operating through his agents in the field, he acquired collections unprecedented in England of marbles, inscriptions, paintings, books, coins and other antiquities, over three decades marked by tireless correspondence and negotiation. At times he imported crateloads of objects from Italy or the Levant without knowing exactly what they contained, willing always to put himelf to the Herculean task of sorting, interpreting, and displaying his treasures. Arundel spent himself and his fortune with such passion, even with such recklessness, as to leave him ultimately bankrupt. His estate was so badly impaired upon his death in 1646—a political refugee in Padua—that most of his collections, especially the paintings, were sold off by his widow to repay his debts.

With no less energy than he devoted to filling his galleries, Arundel also distinguished himself by assembling a remarkable entourage of talented clients and encouraging them in their varied endeavors by his patronage. His artworks—save for the Arundel Marbles, donated by the Earl's grandson to Oxford after the Restoration, and now in the Ashmolean

Museum—were scattered beyond hope of any full scholarly reconstruction. Only sketchy inventories testify to his holdings. Arundel House in the Strand is gone, along with the two-storey long gallery designed by Inigo Jones for Arundel's paintings and statues. Two portraits by Daniel Mytens, of the Earl seated at the threshold of his sculpture galley, and of the Countess seated at the threshold of the picture gallery on the floor below, now hang in Arundel Castle as the only record of those long-gone rooms (fig.1 and 2).

But the other collection for which Arundel was responsible, the corporate work of the Arundelians, remains intact. Of those who enjoyed his patronage, some, like the antiquarians Sir William Dugdale and Sir Robert Cotton, the mathematician William Oughtred, the polymath and legal scholar John Selden, and the philologist Franciscus Junius were better known then than now. Others of more enduring celebrity—Anthony Van Dyck, Inigo Jones, Henry Peacham, and Arundel's personal physician, William Harvey—have made their way into catalogues, monographs and general histories of the formation of the various intellectual and professional disciplines in early modern England. For literary historians, thanks largely to the work of Stephen Orgel and Roy Strong, only Inigo Jones shares the fame of a Donne or a Jonson. Yet taken together, no more brilliant assemblage of talents than those surrounding Arundel existed anywhere in England at the time or, perhaps, since.

These men are, however, inevitably recalled more for their distinctive achievements than for their associations with one another or for their participation in a shared local culture fostered by Arundel—the common ground I hope to reclaim in this book. The recent critical insistence on questioning the boundaries between text and context, and thus on seeking to identify discursive continuities beneath individual performances, has not rooted out our penchant for highlighting outstanding individuals against a more or less indistinct background from which they are said to "stand out." So natural has this procedure seemed, especially in Anglo-American scholarship, that we lack the tools to measure collaborative effort precisely, especially when the participants are practicing in different fields. Disciplinary proprieties still discourage vagrant journeys outside the area of one's specialization, while the ghost of the *Zeitgeist* invoked in such formulas as "Caroline England" or an

"Age of Arundel" seems insufficiently specific as a guide to critical procedures. Especially when hard evidence of personal associations and influences is sparse (as it must be in the record of this period), we feel hesitant in asserting that Van Dyck "must have" had discussions about art with Junius while they were under the same roof and each carrying out Arundel's commissions, including a portrait of the Junius by the artist—although it would be just as hard to imagine that these two Dutchmen studiously avoided each other's company.

Scholarship has thus tended to see the Arundelians' work mainly in the long view, as parts of the discrete disciplinary histories or artistic traditions to which they severally belonged, or which, indeed, they would come to define. For the art historian, Van Dyck's companions include Rubens, Velázquez and the other notables of the European baroque. His English portraits fit into the account of a brief but astonishingly productive career—the artist died at forty—that includes the portraits and religious paintings of his periods in Italy and Antwerp. The painter's relation to Arundel is necessarily subordinated to that broader affiliation. Henry Peacham's *The Complete Gentleman* stands in the line connecting earlier books of advice to princes and aristocratic conduct literature such as Castiglione's *Book of the Courtier* with later bourgeois educational and self–help treatises. The fact that he reserves special praise for Arundel, who in crucial ways serves as Peacham's model, is taken as incidental in this account.

Another Arundelian, the physician William Harvey, enters the history of physiology as the discoverer of the circulation of the blood. Like Vesalius he is hailed as a pioneer of early modern science for his dogged empirical researches and for his refusal to be bound by ancient orthodoxies. Work that appears to have no direct connection to his great discovery—Harvey's more recondite investigations into the sex lives of Arundel's deer, for example, or the interest in art that he shares with his patron—tends to drop out of the record. Harvey himself would doubtless feel vindicated to be known to posterity as the father of modern cardiology rather than solely as a consulting physician to the great. But his connection with Arundel and with the ideas circulating in the Arundelian world of the 1630s cannot be separated from his other achievements.

Of the two polymaths in Arundel's employ, the legal scholar John

Selden published, among many other learned works, the *Marmora Arundeliana* (1628), a digest of the classical inscriptions in the Earl's collection. The other, with whom I will be particularly concerned in this book, is Arundel's librarian, Franciscus Junius the Younger, son of a noted Biblical scholar and nephew of the Leiden humanist Gerardus Vossius. For his contributions to Old English and Gothic philology, Junius has proved indispensable to specialists in medieval studies. One of the principal surviving collections of Anglo-Saxon texts still bears his name as the *Junius Manuscript*, although few Anglo-Saxonists are aware of his other interests or of the importance of his connection to Arundel. Junius is also given a respectful footnote in the history of artistic theory for his treatise on *The Painting of the Ancients*, first published in Latin in 1637 and then in his own English translation the following year.

This work, undertaken at Arundel's behest, broadened the scope of Selden's annotations in the *Marmora* into an exhaustive compendium of classical *dicta* on painting and sculpture, and so provided a scholarly framework for Arundel's antiquities. Praised by Rubens, Junius's book enjoyed a wide European reputation and remained the standard reference on the visual arts in antiquity until the appearance of Winckelmann's *Geschichte der Kunst der Alterthums* in 1764. Even though *The Painting of the Ancients* continued to be cited with some regularity for many years, after Lessing's dismissal of Junius in the *Laocoön* of 1766 for his predecessor's "confusion" of poetry and painting, histories of aesthetics have had only faint praise to the book, regarding it either as one whose theoretical deficiencies were destined to be corrected by more percipient critics, or as a source merely useful in its day for all the Greek and Latin passages it conveniently makes available to painters. In this attenuated history, no one since the seventeenth century has undertaken to recover a sympathetic reading of the book in its own terms, or to explore what it reveals about Arundelian culture in the immediate circumstances of its composition. Thus a "thick" description of the founding moment in the European historiography of ancient art has yet to be written.

Disparate as these Arundelians are in their individual pursuits, they may also be regarded—and it will be my argument that they should be regarded—as contributors to a joint venture. As an index to broader cultural concerns, the common themes and implications of their work go well beyond any one person's horizon, but their projects all bear the impress of Arundel's enthusiasms and, many, of his personal involvement. I propose to look at this body of work at its origin rather than in its consequences. I want to examine it—or at least, some of its crucial features—before its various strands are pulled out and woven into later discourses and detached reputations, and before its immediate patronage context comes unraveled.

The advantage of this re-entanglement is that it brings into view the convergences of thought, the synaptic pathways between ideas, images, forms, and genres that would ultimately disappear from their subsequent histories. The approach is etiological: it explains how things came to be, and it is undertaken in the hope that such insights may lead to a fuller appreciation of what they were to become for us. What may be lost in my approach—for example, a fuller consideration of Junius's influence on European art and art theory, and his eventual role as a foil for Lessing in the 18th-century debate about poetry and painting—may be found in the work of other scholars. I am concerned rather with the formation of an Arundelian cultural poetics as a group enterprise. My aim is to collate the portraits of the Earl by Van Dyck; with Junius's history of the visual arts in antiquity; with the medical researches of Harvey; and ultimately with the relation of these projects to Arundel's antiquarian interests and his (less well known) colonial ambitions, in the light of which these diverse projects are all reflected.

This, then, is an inquiry into what binds the Arundel circle at a particular moment in the 1630s, not a survey of all its members or a pre-history of their influence, but a sounding of their common cultural origin. A brief comment will situate my own approach within the field of patronage studies. In the keynote to an important collection of essays on *Patronage in the Renaissance* published nearly twenty years ago, Werner L. Gundesheimer proposed the broadest possible framework for further research into this fundamental institution of the early modern period:

> [Patronage] has been clearly established as one of the dominant social processes of pre-industrial Europe. It is virtually a permanent structural characteristic of all early European material high culture, based as it is on production by specialists. The effects of patronage are also pervasive in such diverse areas as appointments to secular and religious offices, the conception and creation of the structures and spaces within which people work, pray, and live;

> the execution of the artifacts of material and intellectual culture; the system of transactions into which the behavior of social groups--families, clans, guilds, classes (whether economic, social, occupational, or sexual)—is organized, and through which the relationships of such groups to one another are expressed. Though for scholarly purposes we normally tend to use the term in more limited senses appropriate to the analytical objectives of our particular disciplines, it is important to recognize that particular patrons, and individual acts of patronage of all kinds and degrees, should be understood not only within their own immediate cultural context. They may also be subsumed within a more encompassing theory concerning the systematic effects of patronage in European social and intellectual history.

To "develop such a theory," Gundesheimer concluded even more dauntingly, "would require sophistication and skill in applying to an enormous mass of historical data concepts derived from the various social science disciplines. One can at best hold this up as a long-term goal of collective scholarship" (3–4).Given the alternative between a microscopic and a panoramic view of the subject—between "particular patrons" and "individual acts of patronage" on the one hand, and an "encompassing theory" on the other—prudence dictates a model for patronage studies focused in the middle distance. It seems hardly surprising that no general theory of patronage has emerged in the twenty years since Gundesheimer wrote. To be sure, subsequent studies of individual writers have attempted to sketch in abroader patronage framework. So, for example, in the English context, Robert C. Evans's *Ben Jonson and the Poetics of Patronage* sees Jonson's poems as the "micropolitical performances" of a poet "seeking to advance himself in a society permeated by the psychology of patronage relations" (11)—indeed, by a "psychological system" so pervasive as to suggest that "nearly every work written during the time might be, in some sense, a poem of patronage" (28).

While historians recently convened in order to elaborate the specific bases for such a system "accept that concepts of clientage and patronage are essential to an understanding of early modern European society and politics, "there," as the conveners note, "unanimity ends" (Giry-Deloison 243). So varied are the ramifications of patronage in Gundesheimer's own account that a theory broad enough to "encompass" it would have to be nothing less than theory of Renaissance culture itself, high and low, economic and artistic, a phenomenon of the city as well as the court (see

Archer), and extending its reach into every corner of early modern life, political, ecclesiastical, military, and sexual. However, to focus on a patronage *circle* such as Arundel's—one centered in the ethos of a powerful patron at a particular moment, but defined as well by the variety of interests and projects radiating from it—significantly extends the circumference of the inquiry: not globally "encompassing" in its scope, but ample enough to reveal something of the "conception" of cultural spaces, the production of material artifacts, and the "system of transactions" organizing Arundel's world. If not limitless in its horizon, such a middle view may succeed at least in avoiding the blinckered nominalism to which Gundesheimer objects in "particular" studies.

Thus, although the chapters that follow will take up one or another individual within the Arundel circle, the tool of choice in my discussion is comparison rather than distinction—the appropriate means toward the end of tracing a network of influences and shared assumptions, and the means that alike guards against writing such narratives of untrammeled individual accomplishment as those alluded to above. In the process of collating these Arundelian materials, my working assumption about their interrelationship nonetheless stops short of attempting to merge them all into a single "text." The primal Foucauldian urge to dig down to an undifferentiated discursive stratum underlying all individual utterances is a temptation to be avoided—at least insofar as such an archaeology of knowledge, when it confronts works of visual art and literary texts, will tend to obscure differences in kind that the Renaissance thought it important to preserve.

Jeffrey T. Schnapp has recently warned of the dangers of the "Art/Lit combine," a critical machine too often "employed as a kind of mulching device that shreds every visual and verbal artifact into the same homogenized mulch of images and signs, so that, for instance, films can be read as if they were novels, language-based theorizations transposed over to pictures, bodies treated as texts, three-dimensional objects reduced to flat simulacra" (38). Rereading Foucault's influential discussion of Magritte's pipe, Schnapp argues that what tends to get mulched in *Ceci N'est Pas Un Pipe* is the historical and representational contingency of art objects, indeed the "mystery of objects" themselves, as well as "that dimension in which a pipe is only a pipe, an ordinary object endowed with everyday use-value and a history that is at once private and public" (39).

However great the distance to Magritte from the Arundelian portraitists Van Dyck and Mytens, their painted images of paintings, sculpture and other antiquities in the Earl's collection present us with objects both mysterious and commodified. Indeed such early modern images can be said to define the category of the *objet d'art* that itself forms part of the history of Magritte's "pipe" which is "not a pipe"—the object of a playfully paradoxical meditation balanced on the edge, and dependent on the difference, between the material reality of pipes in the world and their value in, and as, works of art. I want, as well, to respect the distinctiveness of forms and the proper study of those forms—a Van Dyck portrait is a not the "same" as a treatise by Junius—while still highlighting their points of attachment as they articulate similar issues over the ground of their difference.

Nor am I so much concerned with the dissemination of power through the Arundel network as I might be if I were to follow the path of a number of new historicist studies of this period stemming, once more, from the example of Foucault. Insofar as my work deals with patronage, place, the subject (in both senses) and—in my keynote discussion of Madagascar in chapter one—the formation of an early modern colonialist mentality in relation to the courtly culture, as well as to the passion for antiquities, represented by Arundel, I hope that this book will deepen the perspectives opened by the new historicism over the past twenty years. However, it does not try to locate itself in any of the several camps associated with this broad movement.

It seems to me, as it has to others now privileged to look back with hindsight at a whole generation of "new" historicist cultural criticism, that categories have tended to dominate texts and lead to unsurprising conclusions. Too often discussion has been devoted to a tension or opposition in the work of art between the official and the transgressive, between the tendency to promulgate and subvert its informing ideologies, and its (generally coercive) role in the power games of Renaissance culture. I take it as a given that everything surrounding the life of a man so importantly placed at court, so rich, and so influential as Arundel is inseparable from power politics of a very intense voltage—power represented, projected, subverted, and contained, power in relation to the monarch, to clients and, presumably, to the colonial subjects Arundel imagined falling under his sway in Madagascar. I go on from there to ask what else might be interesting to look at in the surviving evidence of this extraordinary community, from which, in a Baconian spirit, any unprefabricated investigation should begin. My goal is the writing of a more open cultural and aesthetic criticism—open to unpredicted connections and imaginings—that tries to see events and their artistic representations copiously, without the restriction of any programmatic set of expectations and results.

As Dustin Griffin has noted in a recent study of literary patronage in 18th-century England (16), a potentially fruitful theoretical perspective can be opened by way of Pierre Bourdieu's analysis of "symbolic capital" in "archaic economies." Bourdieu argues that the limitations of our own post-Marxist assumptions about what constitutes economic activity tend to blind anthropologists to the economic structures implied in the exchange of gifts in traditional cultures assumed not yet to have developed systems of economic exchange recognizable as such to us. What may appear to be—indeed, what presents itself as—the disinterested and "free" exchange of gifts in such cultures is in fact the product of a "guaranteed misrecognition," a necessary concealment "intended to transmute, by the sincere fiction of a disinterested exchange, the inevitable, and inevitably interested relations imposed by kinship, neighbourhood, or work, into elective relations of reciprocity" (Bourdieu 171).

We may, in turn, think of such early modern patronage circles as Arundel's, not as archaic economies but, analogously, as "economies" that have not yet emerged into a kind of modern transparency that would allow us to see the relationships among their members as, in Evans's phrase, "grounded in the self-interest of relatively autonomous individuals operating within a 'free-market' environment" (Evans 25). Bourdieu's critique of the anthropologist's unexamined theoretical assumptions would then prompt us to see in a patronage culture governed by such traditional "symbolic" relations as gratitude, gift-giving, honor, condescension, and emulation, the need to conceal its own economic motivation even from itself—but a need, at that moment, all the more difficult to sustain in the fact of the overtly economic enterprise inseparable from all of Arundel's patronage of the arts. Such a system under strain—an archaic investment in "misrecognition" challenged by an impinging recognition of the market arena in which such gestures were played out—would offer a broader theoretical model for a Marxist reading of early modern patronage. In the case of Arundel, the same perspective helps to explain Junius's need, in *The Painting of the Ancients*, to establish the acquisition of classical art not as an economic transaction but as a cultural translation—as a process of the patron's repossessing what is by right of his own knowledge and virtue already his "own."

At the same time, however, Bourdieu might well lead us to curb our more sweeping theoretical ambitions, or at least to make us aware of the need for a "theory of the *theorization effect*" itself as a condition of our efforts (178; emphasis his). As his title, the *Outline of a Theory of Practice*, suggests, Bourdieu's fundamental argument is that such archaic cultural forms as gift giving (and, we might argue, early modern patronage) are in fact forms of *practice* which cannot be derived from, or subsumed by, an abstract theory that situates itself at an explanatory distance from the evidence it confronts. Indeed it has been the very urge to make presumptive theoretical distinctions between "capital" and the (merely) "symbolic" capital of other cultures that has led to our own misrecognition of their underlying economic function. An intrinsic understanding of practice, including our own critical practices, would call for cultural practices themselves to be understood in a theoretical dimension of their own. It is for this reason that I find it congenial to ally Bourdieu's skepticism of encompassing theories with a sense of Baconian restraint, preferring to trace a network of patronage practices without, in the first instance, feeling the need to apply external theoretical supports.

If I might recur to an older term that Milton uses to combine the intentions of commemorating and reconstructing a fragmented past, I should say that, like Junius facing the scattered remnant of classical commentary on the visual arts, I also aim at "remembering," rather than critically dissecting, a long dismembered body of work. Other terms, such as that envisaging a "sympathetic" connection between distant objects, will emerge from the Arundelians themselves in the course of this study. My own interests are centered both in a small learned circle and, concentrically, in the expanding worlds, past and future, encompassed respectively by Arundel's antiquarian and colonial ambitions. For

Arundel, these two worlds, and the two sorts of ambition that open our vistas onto them, are intimately connected in ways that we have not fully understood as, from our own vantage point, we pursue the history of early colonial thinking in England, or again, the history of classical scholarship during the same period, as distinct subjects. Selden, however, draws together the two realms of intellectual and geographical discovery, which alike "are diligently sought to be possessed by mankind." Echoing a Baconian confidence in the advancement of learning as a voyage of intellectual exploration, Selden believes "all isles and continents" are "so seated, that there is none, but that, from some shore of it, another may be discovered." He continues, in a passage quoted (and emended) by T.K. Woolf, "Certainly the severed [*sic*: several?] parts of good arts and learning, have that kind of site" (qtd. Woolf 35). I will want to suggest below that "severed" is very likely what Selden meant.

The scholarship on Arundel is not voluminous. Mary Hervey's *Life* appeared in 1921 and has never been superseded as a basic resource. It establishes a solid chronology and, quoting amply from his correspondence, allows the Earl to be heard in his own voice as he writes about his ambitions and acquisitions, and ultimately under the shadow of civil war, about ill health, dashed hopes, and exile abroad. An informative chapter on Arundel, from which I have quoted a passage above, appears in Graham Parry's *The Golden Age restor'd* (1981). Yet despite the work done in various fields since 1980 on Renaissance patrons and the culture of the court, surprisingly only one book has been devoted to this crucial figure, David Howarth's *Lord Arundel and his Circle* (1985). As an account of Arundel's career as a collector, it is meticulous if sometimes speculative in its detail, and fulsome in its illustrations. Howarth touches upon nearly everyone known to have come into Arundel's orbit, working with a much broader brush than mine and from the point of view of an art historian. For this reason his book has been invaluable to me, and I have not attempted to surpass it or to write a new life of Arundel.

My own emphasis is on some of the outstanding members of the Arundel circle more than on Arundel directly. My aim has been to focus more closely than Howarth, and from my own perspective as a student of literature, on a selection of particularly rich texts and images. I have paused to meditate on the details and implications of certain key works that tend to get treated in a more summary fashion in more general histories of Stuart culture. In this way I hope to trace the less conspicuous threads by which these examples are woven into recognizable and recurrent patterns, enabling us to read one in terms of the other, to the more complete understanding of the whole.

This design has only gradually suggested itself to me. My original aim was to concentrate on a reading of Junius's *Painting of the Ancients* not only as a pioneering work in the history of art but as a work of imaginative literature constructing the very history it records. Fortuitously a new, copiously annotated edition of Junius's writings on art appeared in 1991 (see Aldrich), the first edition to be published since 1694, with the exception of a 1972 facsimile of *The Painting of the Ancients*. But there has never been a critical book on Junius, and on *The Painting of the Ancients* itself, although the work is often noted as having been broadly influential, there have been only a few articles to my knowledge, notably a dense chapter in Allan Ellenius's *De Arte Pingendi* (1960) summarizing Junius's theories and relating them to the development of a Latin art literature in Sweden in the later seventeenth century; a 1983 essay in French by Colette Nativel analyzing the rhetorical structure of the argument; and an essay in German by Martin Warnke, published in 1991, on Junius's view of history. My debt to these scholars will appear in what follows, but none does what seems to me is needed from the point of view of the Arundel circle. That original intention remains as the basis for my chapters on Junius below.

It soon became clear, however, that in spite of the appeal of a topic so untrodden and so neatly delimited, Junius could not be understood fully except when his work was collated with that of the other Arundelians. What was Junius's motivation at a certain moment in undertaking such a book, the first of its kind, a history of the plastic arts in antiquity? That he was encouraged to pursue such researches by Arundel as part of his own enterprise as a collector of antiquities only deepens the question and points outward to others directly or indirectly involved in it. Histories such as Junius's are always about the past but for the present. What contemporary interests does his book reflect, designate, and authorize by its re-collection of the Ancients?

This was not simply a matter of placing Junius in his contemporary framework, but of the attempt at much more fundamental and detailed integration. The answers lead us to correlate history, antiquities, painting, poetry, patronage, colonization and collecting among other activities associated with Arundel, and to see their bearing on the intellectual coordinates of Arundel's England. I might note one other part of my design that only gradually came into view. Having thought to dispose of the two most interesting portraits we have of Arundel in my chapter on Madagascar—the Van Dyck "Madagascar" portrait of the Earl seated with a globe of the world (fig. 3), and the Mytens, mentioned above, showing him seated before his sculpture gallery—I found myself coming back to them through the eyes of Junius, and again in light of my discussion of "sympathy" and "circulation" in the chapter Harvey, each time noticing something new, or some new way of thinking about what I had seen before. In this way, my movement around the circle leads me back to these two endlessly fascinating pictures as one touchstone of the whole enterprise.

In their broadest form, a crucial set of insights provided by Junius's text in relation to Arundel respond to the wish expressed at the beginning of Andrew Marvell's "To His Coy Mistress." What if we really *had* "world enough and time"—not only the time for such an aristocratic indulgence as art collecting, or for writing books on ancient painting, but time itself, past and future, as a joint possession along with an expanding world? This is a theme I will want to develop more fully below, but it might be noted here that the Caroline world, as the Arundelians knew it, already extended westward to the Americas and eastward at least as far as the "Indian Ganges' side," where Marvell imagines his Coy Mistress finding rubies, and where the East India Company had more palpable designs on cotton, dyes, silk, pepper, teak, ebony, and sugar, as well as diamonds and rubies from the famed mines at Golconda.

In the "cultural geography of the court," to borrow Malcolm Smuts' phrase (104), Arundel connects the royal center—where as Earl Marshall he had an important "place"—with the periphery of the wider world toward whose far-flung places his ambition as a collector and, briefly, as the sponsor of a colony, drew him. The ambiguity of "place" in contemporary usage is a fruitful one for mapping the poles of the world Arundel spans. It can mean both a geographical locale and a position within a patronage system at court—a place in which, not coincidentally, authority was directly proportional to one's spatial relation to the King, with the greatest influence exercised by those few who had access to the most private places, the royal Bedchamber and the Privy Chamber. It can also designate the commonplaces of a text.

Thomas More had located his utopian fiction along the same two coordinates of "place" more than a century before. The center is occupied by the character called "More," who like Arundel serves the court, and who in the debate of Book I argues for participating in civic affairs. His opponent and alter ego in that debate, the sunburned philosophical absolutist Raphael Hythloday, haunts the periphery whence he returns with his account of the Utopians. Hythloday is a "stranger" and one estranged from all obligations. He speaks for a part of More, and a part of Arundel, "freely ranging," as Sidney would say of the poet, "within the zodiac of his own wit" (216). Located somewhere at the outer reaches of the world, Utopia is an island like England, but one established by the negation of everything held to be positive in More's world, like money, private property, and courtly service. For the England of 1516 this place was "noplace," an Erasmian wise folly but a folly nonetheless.

By the 1630s, with the glories of empire still in the future but with a scattering of English settlements in the new world and a growing trade with the east, distant places had begun to take on a more substantial reality. What survives of *Utopia* in the English geographical imagination is not only the configuration of space between central and peripheral "places," both reflecting and yet radically different from each other. New places tend to strike the observer as uncanny—inextricably familiar and strange, and, as More learns from Hythloday, they may prove to be very old. From More's text also comes the imagined conflation of literary "places" and concrete "places." A letter from Peter Giles to Jerome Busleiden printed with the *Utopia* facetiously considers the question of the location of the island, about which a number of More's readers were allegedly curious. Giles observes that it is eminently worthy of study as an island "superior to" or "far beyond" Plato's *Republic* (*ut plusquam Platonicam*) (*Works* 20). Does Utopia surpass Plato's republic in its excellence (as an ideal place, a fictional construct), or does it lie in a more remote part of the world? Here Plato's *Republic*, containing the sketch of an ideal republic, and the putatively real island of Utopia (which we are allowed to forget for the moment has no existence outside More's *Utopia*) slide effortlessly into the same imaginative commonplace where (ancient) literary texts and (new) geographical realities coincide.

Thus, the distance in space that separates England from Utopia also marks the expanse of time that separates Hythloday from Plato, to whom he is compared as a philosophical traveler. As a latter-day version of the one in the *Republic* who has returned to the cave with a vision of the truth—he who has seen the sun but who strikes those living in the shadows as speaking nonsense—Hythloday has his historical origin in Plato, just as he has his geographical destination in Utopia. Utopian life has remained largely unchanged for 1760 years. To the extent that this ancient world, now rediscovered, embodies a program for social reform, it also serves as a blueprint for the future. More's narrative locates itself at the same intersection of history and cartography that we will find in Van Dyck's "Madagascar" portrait of Arundel. In this founding narrative of exploration (Hythloday had sailed with Amerigo Vespucci), More anticipates not only the colonial projects of the next age, but the intellectual and artistic projects of the Arundelians, as well as the actual voyages of Arundel's agents in search of the fragments of a past with which they could return to England. "The mind is its own place," as Satan will observe: a psychological domain, a social position, a location in the world. One of my main themes will have to do with the attempt at a cultural suturing of these several places, the Arundelians looking back to old worlds and out to new, to other places from whose distant vantage point one's own might be plotted.

This book is divided into four chapters. The first focuses on the collaboration of Arundel and Anthony Van Dyck in imagining a project much on the Earl's mind as the clouds of civil war gathered in the late 1630s, a colonizing expedition to the island of Madagascar. It is no coincidence that the artist's "Madagascar" portrait of the Earl and Countess displays a sampling of Arundel's antiquities along side the globe on which the site of the future settlement is indicated (fig. 3). Both the colony and the antiquities are Arundel's possession—as is the globe itself, which thus mediates between the material objects in the Earl's collection and the distant worlds they represent. The Van Dyck portrait reveals the interplay among a number of themes that (together with the painting itself in its role in the promotion of Arundel's scheme) configure an art of colonization.

The two following chapters read Junius's *The Painting of the Ancients*, commissioned by Arundel three years earlier, as the antiquarian counterpart of the "Madagascar" portrait. Junius's book is most simply, and most tellingly, described as a kind of *cento*—a compendium of virtually every passage commenting on the visual arts that the indefatigable philologist could find in the *corpus* of ancient writing. As such, it figures both as a "collection" of texts and an attempt (like Arundel's) to fit the fragments of a lost artistic tradition into a coherent narrative. Like the "Madagascar" portrait, it had its immediate and practical use in the furtherance of Arundel's designs, in the case of Junius's book as a *vade mecum* to the antiquities market as well as an encyclopedic framework into which his patron's various acquisitions could be fit. A collection in its own right, it also represents a massive act of re-collection, not only a scholarly memorial to ancient art but the construction of what it memorializes. This founding moment in the historiography of classical art allows us to see, from Junius's point of view, the process by which the mind, in making the past its own, rationalizes both the antiquarian's relation to antiquity and the colonialist's dream of distant possessions. This liaison between two Arundelian projects helps to explain the presence of a figure identified as Junius in one version of the "Madagascar" portrait (fig. 4).

The last chapter turns to the medical arts as practiced by Sir Kenelm Digby and, more famously in the annals of medicine, by the Earl's personal physician William Harvey. In the 1630s Digby was perhaps more celebrated in medical circles than his great contemporary as the proponent of a cure-all dubbed "The Powder of Sympathy," a marvelous compound which was supposed to heal injuries at a distance from the wounded individual—from across the room, perhaps even from across the world. The nostrum was, of course, worthless. But at the heart of Digby's fascination with its reputed powers lay a truly powerful figure for the bridging of distances and an "explanation" of the way in which one substance could affect another with no apparent direct contact between them. The chimera of a "sympathetic" connection between distant objects informs and naturalizes a therapeutic bond between the would-be colonial proprietor and his distant possession, as well as that between the collector of antiquities and their origin in remoteness of the ancient world. Harvey himself would fall back on a theory of sympathy to explain the otherwise mysterious origin of life at the moment of conception. His experiments in embryology as well his discovery of the circulatory system are based on reimagining the little world of the body in ways consonant with the other worlds, old and new, that compelled the attention of the Arundel circle. His speculation on the mysteries of "conception," in turn, folds back into Mytens's conception of Arundel's paternal relation to the statues in his gallery.

A brief conclusion on *The Tempest* recasts Arundel in the role of Prospero—as magus, conservator of memory, exile, and governor of an island. Assuming the strong likelihood that Arundel actually saw the play during its production at court in the winter of 161–613, it refocuses our critical perspective on the *The Tempest* as a prophetic protocolonial fantasy from the viewpoint of the "Collector" Earl.

I want, finally, to be very clear about the way in which the word *circle* is intended in the title of this book, and in the following chapters. In the most specific sense, we think of an artistic, scientific, or social circle as comprised of a group of like-minded individuals whose common interests bring them together on a more or less regular basis, whether casually or under the auspices of a formal institution dedicated to those interests. Convivial evenings passed at the Mermaid tavern by young poets who thought of themselves as the "sons of Ben" would be an example of the former, as would, eventually, the coffee-house circles of the eighteenth century. After the Restoration, the Royal Society would be an example of the latter. Somewhere between these two would be the literary circles, such as that with which "Jack" Donne is associated, centered on the Inns of Court.

Aristocratic patronage circles differ from these insofar as they center on an individual—Bess of Hardwick, Lucy, Countess of Bedford, Mrs. Magdalene Herbert—upon whom their members are to some degree dependent for support and recognition. Their "members" may come and go. They may fall into favor and out of favor, and the relations between them may be slight except for their mutual connection to the patron. Nor is there any reason to assume that the work they do as part of the circle will bear a common stamp other than the patron's approval. The Arundel circle was closer-knit, for the two reasons suggested above. Arundel, a man of determined purpose with deep scholarly and artistic interests of his own, directly shaped the projects undertaken at his behest. We know that he commissioned Junius's work on ancient art, and there can be little doubt that he designed the program for the Madagascar portrait in detail, personally composing or approving the setting in which he would be painted by Van Dyck. Second, Arundel maintained a long and close connection with his favored clients. Junius lived in his house for over twenty years; Harvey conducted his experiments in animal vivisection at Arundel Castle and accompanied the Earl on his travels; and Arundel appears not only to have been instrumental in bringing Van Dyck to England but remained his most important patron aside from King Charles until the artist's death. Such ties make it plausible to speak of these three at least as engaged in a common enterprise whose different facets all reflect the movement of Arundel's mind.

A full exploration of this collaborative work warrants bringing others more tangential to this immediate group into the discussion. Thus the publication by Davenant of a long poem on Madagascar a year before the commission of the Madagascar portrait helps to account for the painting, and also for Arundel's unlikely interest—more imaginative than realistically economic—in that part of the world (Davenant's *Madagascar* is discussed in the Appendix). Harvey provides a model of "circulation" writ large in Arundel's artistic commerce with the ancient world. By the same token, Digby's pseudoscientific theory of a "sympathetic" cure becomes pertinent in the light of Harvey's appeal to its reasoning in his explanation of the mysteries of fertility, and, in turn, of our understanding of Arundel's "sympathetic" connection to antiquity.My own critical procedure, like Donne's in "A Valediction: Forbidding Mourning," will be to describe the circle. The one foot of my critical compass remains fixed on Arundel at the center, while the main sweep of the narrative moves through Van Dyck, Junius and Harvey. It is all the more important, therefore, to state straightforwardly at the outset the thesis circulating through this analysis. Arundel's central importance to this book is that he combines in himself, and through the projects he sponsors, the dual role as a colonial visionary and a collector of antiquities. These two interests would seems to pull in different directions, towards a past long gone and a future yet to be. In fact, for Arundel, the two are joined. Moving centripetally, I want to show how this conjunction helps us to understand the texts and images at hand. Moving centrifugally, I want to show how this coincidence of opposites, so clearly visible in the Arundel circle, is more broadly symptomatic of English national self-consciousness in the 1630s.

1. Madagascar on My Mind: Arundel, Van Dyck and the Arts of Colonization

On a round ball
A workeman that hath copies by, can lay
An Europe, Afrique, and an Asia,
And quickly make that, which was nothing, *All*

John Donne, "A Valediction: of Weeping" (38, ll 10–12)

In the autumn of 1639, Thomas Howard, Earl of Arundel and Surrey, was ill in health, virtually bankrupt, and embittered by the recent course of political events. Having led the King's armies into Scotland, he returned from the First Bishops' War after a punishing campaign and the conclusion of what many of Charles's supporters could only regard as an ignominious peace. The debts awaiting Arundel at home were mounting toward one hundred thousand pounds, much of it expended on the collection of antiquities. Reduced nearly to nothing, he turned all his thoughts to Madagascar. Perhaps his hope lay in the east. With a ship provided by the King and an ample fund to be raised by the sale of stock to fellow "Adventurers," might he not repair his fortunes by planting a colony on that favored isle off the Afrique coast? My discussion will focus on these two apparently unrelated ventures: Arundel's brief, abortive scheme—long forgotten—to establish an English colony on Madagascar, and his long, spectacularly fruitful if ultimately ruinous career as a collector of antiquities, for which he is justly renowned. My principal object of study will be Anthony Van Dyck's "Madagascar" portrait of Arundel, completed in the autumn of that same year of 1639 (fig. 3), in which these two projects are combined. The context of my discussion includes several other paintings and documents produced by the members of the Arundel circle that shed light on on this particular convergence, but I am ultimately concerned with the broader question of the relation between "old" and "new" knowledge of the world at this exemplary moment in the early modern history of English exploration and colonial ambition.

In Arundel's lifetime, the expansion of geographical frontiers in every direction of the compass was matched by a like expansion in the scope of knowledge, which "by the early seventeenth century had burst the bounds of the library" and challenged ancient truths on every front (Grafton 3). Mariners' reports, travelers' accounts, the "advancement of learning" in the arts of navigation and cartography, the telescopic observations of the heavens and the anatomical explorations of the human body—all promised fresh stocks of knowledge about the world. The fruits of such intellectual daring reassured the Baconians, if not a more skeptical Donne, that the mind's dominion over nature would expand apace. At the same time, as recent work in various fields has shown, "old" patterns of thought, classical and Biblical, retained much of their power and durability (Mazzola). What we might now characterize as the beginning of a paradigm shift in the conception of knowledge itself, provoked both by an expansion of the "known" world and by the parallel invention of new technologies of intellectual exploration, was as much propelled as impeded by an undercurrent of conventional wisdom. Whether in the expectation that the "new" world might likely harbor Homeric Amazons or lost tribes of Israel, or the allegory of "America" as a buxom maiden reawakened from the slumber of the ages by the European explorer (Montrose 2), or the impression formed by Sandys on his African travels that certain village women were the image of Medean witches out of Ovid (Haynes), the "old" was always, perhaps inevitably, available as a template for (re)conceiving new experience. The persistence of ingrained habits of thought in this (or any) period of abrupt cultural change hardly surprises us. In the realm of natural philosophy we have come to understand, with Kuhn, that the boldest claims of unprecedented invention figure rhetorically within the discourse of science to conceal their implication in ideas since discarded in the name of progress.

The convergence of Arundel's antiquarian and colonial interests in the program of the Madagascar portrait reveals a clear and richly articulated network of connections between the "old" and the "new." Reflecting the collaboration of Van Dyck and his patron in the creation of a colonial ideal, it makes possible a particularly nuanced description of what I will call the imagination of the protocolonial moment in Caroline England. As Donne's "Valediction," quoted above, suggests in its conjunction of mimesis with making, the reproduction of familiar "copies" or patterns with acts of autonomous—even magical—creation *ex nihilo*, the idea of Madagascar at that moment will depend upon the recovery of an image of the past even as it contemplates the foundation of a new colony. This chapter is about the "making" of such an idea within the Arundel circle and, by implication, beyond its circumference.

The prospective voyage would be undertaken, in the ringing tones of the Earl's public "Declaracon concerning Madagascar" of September 6th, 1639, for the "propagacion of Christian Religion and prosecucion of the Eastern Trafficque." He had no doubt that like-minded men would be attracted in great numbers by the "powerfull inducements of honor and profitt," and he directed them to appear, money in hand to guarantee their share, between eight and eleven in the morning, Tuesdays and Fridays, at Arundel House in the Strand (Hervey 506; Howarth 167–68). Surely riches beckoned from an island not only bounteous in itself but strategically located athwart the trade routes linking India, Africa, and the Levant. Yet to Arundel, the idea of Madagascar represented more than a canny investment in an area whose seemingly limitless commercial potential had already been suggested by the successes of the East India Company. Leaving behind his creditors and an England torn by civil strife, Arundel and his company might look forward to the retirement of a tropical paradise. Despite these alluring prospects, the scheme quickly collapsed—perhaps for fear of the Earl's poor health, or perhaps because too few were willing to invest in what Sir Thomas Roe had called the "dreame of Madagascar" (qtd. Hervey 417). Aside from Arundel's own prospectus, Van Dyck's double portrait of the Earl and the Countess is the only surviving record of the abortive venture, the sitters indicating the location of the future colony on a large round ball of the earth.

Van Dyck's painting opens the idea of Madagascar, not simply by recording the event (or non-event) of the Earl's anticipated voyage but by giving it an imaginative shape. It advertises the venture, forms part of its brief history, and epitomizes the cultural matrix within which the Madagascar project figures. My interest lies in pursuing the several apparently disparate, yet finally converging, themes suggested by this image. If Arundel's colonial ambition is at the center of the image, then bound up with it are the interests of portraiture itself, of heraldry, of connoisseurship and the collection of antiquities, and even, as we shall see, of the origins of the discourse of art history. For in one version of the portrait, now at Knole (fig. 4), a figure appears in the background who has been identified as either the Reverend William Petty or as Francis Junius the Younger. Petty was for many years Arundel's chief agent in the eastern antiquities trade. Junius, employed since 1621 as Arundel's librarian and resident philologist, had published his *De Pictura Veterum* in 1637, followed the next year by an English translation of this groundbreaking history of art in antiquity, *The Painting of the Ancients* (London, 1638). Why should these figures be associated with the idea of Magadascar?

The presence of either figure suggests an immediate link between classical art and that of Van Dyck himself, with the further implication of a *paragone* between the ancients and the moderns. In different ways, Petty and Junius are responsible for bringing antiquity to the fore—whether by supplying the "antiquities" represented in the painting itself, or by establishing their historical context. Standing behind Arundel, this figure directs his gaze not at the patron but outward, from the depths of the composition toward the painter. The effect ressembles the self-conscious mirror imagery in Velázquez or Vermeer, intimating in this case both a rivalry and a collaboration in making the antique "visible." The virtual presence of the modern painter in the gaze of his antiquarian counterpart also heightens the role of the painting itself as a signficant artifact, its own beauty and cultural importance rivaling those of the prestigious objects it represents.

In this light, the Madagascar portrait—as the work of Van Dyck—would have been received at the time as more than a disinterested representation. The painter's fame in England, the very assertion that such a subject is worthy of his art, indeed that the meticulously rendered globe, turned so as to display the island of Madagascar and contemplated by Arundel with proprietary interest, has already been conceived and realized by Van Dyck—all this stands as an implicit endorsement of the Earl's project. Van Dyck's celebrity enhances that of his subjects of course, just as their patronage enhances his. But with Arundel the exchange works in subtler ways as well.

Arundel had been influential in attracting Van Dyck to England, his sponsorship of the painter going back perhaps as far as 1620–21 when the twenty-year-old Flemish genius first visited London. After establishing himself permanently in England in 1632, Van Dyck eclipsed all others, including not only Daniel Mytens but even Rubens, as the craftsman of Arundel's image. In 1635 he completed a magnificent portrait of the Earl with his young grandson Thomas, later 5th Duke of Norfolk (fig. 5), to which we shall return. In the Madagascar portrait the artist's authority and that of the would-be colonial administrator converge: the very fact of the painting's commission testifies as much to the Earl's power to command such a notable "workeman" as Van Dyck, as to his own ability to share in the imaginative power of the artist.

In 1633 Van Dyck had already produced a literal vision of the exotic such as might now allure Arundel's imagination: a lush, full-length portrait of William Fielding, Earl of Denbigh, on the sitter's return from a voyage to India and Persia (fig. 6). Denbigh is depicted in Indian dress, fowling-piece in hand. He has just emerged from an unmistakably English landscape to his right, but has now stopped before the improbable scene of a palm tree, a parrot, and a native boy, which seems suddenly to have opened on his left—as if he had just stepped into, and been transformed by, an Indian fantasy. Although parrots and coconuts betoken the riches to be had in the Indies (Hall 232), Denbigh's gaze, like Arundel's in the Madagascar portrait, is directed as much inward as outward, slightly elevated and intensely absorbed. He is not in fact looking at the parrot toward which the boy is trying to direct his attention. As Richard Wendorf observes in his discussion of this work, Denbigh's expression, if marked by a certain disquiet or apprehension like Arundel's, is nonetheless suffused with curiosity, wonder, and a kind of awe evoked from the realm of sacred painting (103), and reminiscent of the marvelous spectacle revealed at the end of an Inigo Jones masque. In this Indian reverie we see what in the Madagascar portrait is unseen but strongly suggested in Arundel's expression: the vision before the mind's eye of a new world unsullied by debts and wars—a sceptered isle under the Earl's own dominion.

In the September 6th declaration of his plan, potential investors are invited to join with Arundel in "soe worthy a designe" (Hervey 506). Arundel's "designe" for Madagascar, like the Platonized *disegno interno* of Mannerist art theory, is the Idea or preconception of the colony, perfect in the inventor's mind and there judged to be "worthy" even before it is embodied in material reality. To adapt the earlier but apposite language of Sidney's *Defence of Poesy*, it is the "*idea* or fore-conceit for the work" in which the skill of the artificer may be seen (216), its enticing narrative of the impending expedition no mere fiction, but an "imaginative ground-plot"—the mind's blueprint or ground plan—"of a profitable invention" (235). The architectural metaphor implicit in Sidney's "ground-plot" (which may also suggest the prepared background of a painting) reinforces the ancient connections between the artistic imagination and the building of civilization. As Sidney reminds us elsewhere in the *Defence*, "Amphion was said to move stones with his poetry to build Thebes," and among the other great foundational poets—Musaeus, Homer, Hesiod, Orpheus—the lawgiver Solon was credited by Plato in the *Timaeus* with having composed a (lost) epic on the (lost) island of Atlantis (213). The added note, in Sidney's memorable phrase, that such an invention is "profitable," in our context takes on a financial as well as a moral inflection.

In the Madagascar portrait, a half-crumpled drawing, draped with apparent casualness over the frame of the globe (we will return to the heraldic content of this drawing below), catches the eye of the viewer. Might it suggest the role of the painting itself, analogous to that of the declaration, as the preliminary sketch for a project (like the "copies" or templates available to the world-making workman in Donne's "Valediction") that now exists as a glimmer in the Earl's imagination? This interior design is just partly revealed in the rapt expression on Arundel's face as he contemplates the idea soon to be given a local habitation and a name on the island of Madagascar. Among the other art objects represented in the portrait, the presence in the background of a bronze head known then as the "Arundel Homer" also reinforces the Earl's connection to the poetry of epic voyages and durable heroic achievement. The fragility of the drawing, however—how easily could a small movement of the globe, a slight gust of air, blow this one out of the picture—may also suggest the fragility of the idea. As we are reminded by the title of Jeffrey Knapp's *An Empire Nowhere,* until fairly late in the history of European colonization, and certainly compared with the successes of Spain and Portugal, England's "empire" outside the British Isles was largely "nowhere," imaginary and utopian (Knapp 1–4). A noplace like the featureless island toward which Arundel gestures in the portrait, Madagascar still awaits the stamp of the Idea for its realization. We shall return to the anachronism of applying to this period of sporadic venturing, piratic expeditions, and failed plantations any notion of "empire," and hence of "imperialism," with any of the later connotations of those words. Indeed, Arundel's September declaration seems to anticipate the skepticism of the potential investor who may regard the project as something like an illusion of Prospero's, for in that document, the money, the ships, Earl's own "Creditt wth the world" and the fact that he plans to go to Madagascar in person, are all offered as evidence to "disabuse such as shall thinke this a vayne & ayrye undertaking" (506).

The subsequent history of Madagascar would, inevitably, devalue the golden world of Arundel's conception to a far harsher, brazen reality, although several enthusiasts kept the vision alive, however vain and airy it may have seemed, into the 1640s. Since the early years of the sixteenth century, first the Portuguese and later the Dutch, the Spanish, and the French had all made forays into the area. On Christmas day, 1601, an English expedition of three ships on route to the spice islands—the first such venture to be launched by the newly-chartered East India Company—stopped for provisions in Madagascar. There, in Antongil Bay on the northeast coast of the island, they learned from an inscription scratched into a rock that five Dutch ships had preceded them in October, and that as many as two hundred Dutch seaman had succumbed to a tropical fever during their brief and tragic visit. In 1636 King Charles considered sending an expedition to the island, over which he somewhat prematurely appointed his nephew Prince Rupert of the Palatinate, then only seventeen, as Viceroy. Rupert's own mother, Elizabeth, concerned that her son was getting swept up by the "Romance" of the idea that he might "Don Quixotte-like conquer that famous island," wrote to Sir Thomas Roe imploring him to "put such windmills out of [the Prince's] head" (qtd. in Davenant 343). But Rupert himself seems to have lost interest before long. By mid-1637 Roe was able to reassure Elizabeth, "The dream of Madagascar, I think, is vanished" (qtd. in Davenant 343). The dream nevertheless reappeared in 1643 with the publication of Walter Hamond's *Madagascar: The Richest and Most Fruitful Island in the World*, followed a year later by Richard Boothby's *A Briefe Discovery or Description of the most Famous Island of Madagascar*. Boothby touted the island as "a very Earthly Paradise" and "the chiefest place in the World to enrich men by trade." In 1644, 120 English colonists sailed into the Bay of St. Augustin and built a fort. However, they quickly ran afoul of the local inhabitants, unwisely declining to join them in battle against their tribal enemies. Murder and starvation took all but twelve of the colonists within a year, and the survivors returned to England—leaving "behind them only a ruined fort and a large cemetery" (Heseltine 68–70).

A feeling of melancholy and unease in the painting, the slight apprehension in the faces of the Earl and the Countess, may already convey a prescient awareness that this overreaching venture was destined to fail. A laudatory "Short View" of Arundel's life, written by Sir Edward Walker in 1705, concedes that if the Earl were "defective in anything, it was that he could not bring his Mind to his Fortune; which though great, was far too little for the Vastness of his noble Designs" (Howarth 222). The judgment applies equally to the huge sums lavished by Arundel on his purchase of antiquities, and to the colonial design too vast either for his own fortunes or for those of his chimerical shareholders. For this gap between design and realization, as for a painter like Leonardo who could not finish pictures already perfected in his mind, there is at least the consolation offered by Sidney that "any understanding knoweth the skill of the artificer standeth in that *idea* or fore-conceit of the work, and not in the work itself" (21). Van Dyck's work alone embodies the nascent idea and, as it happened, the graveyard of Arundel's hopes.

In the Madagascar portrait, the stiff twin compasses held by the Countess in her right hand, pointing, like the Earl's index finger and on a line with it, toward the location of the future colony on the globe, also serve to unite the expedition to Madagascar with its representation by Van Dyck, for these are at once the instruments of navigation and artistic composition. Worlds, as the Renaissance knew from Pythagorean and scriptural sources alike, are created in number, weight and measure. As Junius's editors observe of this detail, again in terms that apply equally to the underlying *ratio* of artistic and political design, the compasses "confirm as much the Arundels' commitment to measured order in their resolve to establish the colony as they ensure the safe course of navigation on which the enterprise depends" (Aldrich I, caption to his fig. 11). The motif may also be taken to emblematize the guarantee of the prospectus that in due measure every adventurer will be given "his full and ratable proporcion in the proffitts of the voyage," according to the amount of his initial investment (Hervey 506).

Such a liaison between Arundel and Van Dyck, their imaginative partnership in the Madagascar project, is strengthened by the tendency of Europeans—as Stephen Greenblatt has noted, citing a passage in Peter Martyr—to see colonized regions and their peoples as "rased or vnpainted tables," blank canvasses "apte to receave what formes soo ever [of religion or civilized custom] are fyrst drawen theron by the hande of the paynter" (16). Painters would frequently accompany colonial expeditions to record whatever marvels might be found. From the time of Elyot's *Booke of the Governor* courtiers had been urged to learn at least the rudiments of painting as an adjunct to their military skills, allowing them to make sketches for the purpose of reconnaissance and logistical planning. In the witty allegory of civil war in "Upon Appleton House," Andrew Marvell would survey the meadow of his patron's estate cleared by the mowers with military precision and see in this "leveled space" a "new and empty face of things"—a portrait *in potentia*, a blank canvas prepared for the designers of a new social order like "cloths for [the painter Sir Peter] *Lely* stretched to stain" (ll. 442–444). The winners in the civil war would have their opportunity, however brief, to sketch in their design for a Commonwealth, while Marvell's Fairfax, like Arundel a disillusioned military commander, would retire to cultivate his private gardens. For Arundel, the satisfactions of Amphion could only be found in art. As a collector he could reassemble the stones of an old world. The prospectus for Madagascar allowed him to imagine a new one—in the event, one no less remote and inaccessible as the ancient world whose fragments he preserved. In the compensatory fantasy of the Van Dyck portrait, the painter anticipates rather than accompanies the expedition, heralding it by recording its inception in the idea from which it will (never) be realized, and investing the depicted colonizer with his own artistic mastery of invention and design.

There is, however, a much more specific sense in which Arundel *heralds* the upcoming project, for in the Van Dyck portrait he appears most prominently in his role as Earl Marshall, the chief herald of the realm. While the Earl's right hand points toward the globe along a near-horizontal line, his left seems to steady it from above. In this hand he holds the Earl Marshall's baton, establishing a near-vertical line that seems to pierce the top of the globe like a polar axis. In contrast to the open pointing gesture of the right hand, the left hand is closed, almost clenched around the staff of office so as to suggest the potential power that Arundel has (literally) in his grasp. The golden baton placed into his hand by that of King James might now be used as a lever to turn the very world. The other portraits of Arundel show him to be inseparable from this emblem of the high office he had held since 1621. It is prominently displayed in the 1635 Van Dyck portrait of the Earl and his grandson already mentioned (fig. 5), where the child's gaze draws our attention to the baton as an emblem of paternal discipline: a cane, in effect, that we may regard with something of "Little Tom's" mixed feelings of apprehension and respect. We know, even if the child is too young to understand it, that his own future rests on the security of his grandfather's titles, both symbolized in, and guaranteed by, the baton of the chief heraldic officer of the kingdom. That the Earl himself begins the Madagascar prospectus of 1639 by giving this title the same prominence ("I, Thomas Earle of Arundell and Surrey, Earle Marshall of England") leads us to consider this aspect of his authority more closely. How is the power of this (to us) arcane and curious office enmeshed with that of the artist and the colonialist?

Of the project's "powerful inducements of honor and profitt," it is "honor" that is the special province of the Earl Marshall. He is an honorable man himself, of course, in the moral as well as in the technical sense that he is a gentleman entitled to the honor of bearing arms. To this, in the Madagascar portrait, the drawing visible on the casually draped paper mentioned above offers a kind of visible certification by exhibiting the Earl's heraldic animals and his motto. By virtue of his office he is not only a trustworthy administrator but the guardian of the kingdom's honor as well. As symbolized by the full armor worn by Arundel under his ermine cloak, the Earl Marshall had originally—in the late middle ages—been supreme military commander (Day 98–99). One of his ceremonial duties, joining the worlds of arms and arts, was still to arrange the order of combats in the lists. By Arundel's day, the office having been newly strengthened for him, the Earl Marshall presided over the Court of Chivalry, which had in its purview all matters relating to the honor of a gentleman. Its main function was to legalize and enforce decisions made by the College of Arms, adjudicating contested claims to title and prosecuting alleged infringements of armorial bearings.

Heraldry is thus a judicial and an administrative institution concerned with granting, recording, and securing the legitimacy of coats of arms. Its historical underpinnings are supplied by the polymath John Selden, a member of Arundel's circle. In his *Titles of Honour* (1614), Selden had argued at length that systems of rank and title existed from the beginning as the organizing principle of civil society. His is not a "soft" primitivism like that imagined by Montaigne for his uncorrupted and ungoverned Peruvian cannibals, nor yet a "hard" primitivism like Hobbes's primordial war of all against all. Rather, as Selden's wide-ranging survey of ancient civilizations is intended to prove, the very possibility of social order is embedded in the natural distinctions among men and realized in the "titles of honor" accorded their differing ranks of nobility. Selden's argument would have been strengthened for Arundel by his standing as a legal scholar. The herald's duty to the law, his continuing obligation to the past in which his own authority is rooted, calls for vigilant police work to shore up that ancient institution. In the face of such widespread abuses as the sale of honors to those with weak or disputed claims, even outright fraud in the confection of bogus genealogies (see Falco), heraldic officers dispatched on official visitations throughout the realm were charged with making the most scrupulous investigations of questionable cases. As J.F.R. Day observes, citing the case of an offender who suffered a whipping and the loss of his ears for dispensing counterfeit coats of arms and pedigrees, "Heraldic abuses were considered attacks on the foundation of the state, and were punished accordingly" (98). A man seasoned in this work would have the knowledge to plant a new colony along time-honored lines, the experience justly to dispense its honors and titles—and the power, both to civilize or subdue its aboriginal inhabitants and afterwards to secure its orderly government.

To discriminate between the authentic and the fake, to establish true identities and weed out forgeries and impostors by historical research—these are the requisite skills of the connoisseur as well as the herald. Selden's own pursuit of Oriental manuscripts and his antiquarian work under the patronage of Arundel bring his heraldic and legal talents to bear on the realm of the collector. The author of *Titles of Honor* went on to publish his *Marmora Arundeliana* in 1628, a digest of the ancient inscriptions found on the marbles in Arundel's collections, and one inspiration for Junius's *The Painting of the Ancients* ten years later. In the context of the Madagascar portrait, it is no less important to recall that in its more benign offices, heraldry is also a form of art, involved in the emblematic design of coat armor as well as the orchestration of ceremonial occasions. Despite Ben Jonson's jibe at the pretenses of title in the *Epigrams* ("I a Poet here, no Herald am"), heraldry incorporates a kind of poetics with its own style and the technical terminology of the *blazon*, whose "azure waves" and "sable nights" migrate from the precise stipulation of armorial bearings into the broader stream of poetic language (Day 98–99). In the legal and the poetic sense alike, the herald can be said to "create" both gentlemen and the symbolism in which their titles are registered.

A similar power of denomination is exercised by Arundel and his fellow Renaissance collectors when they simply declare—as was their typical practice—an unidentified statue *to be* a Cicero or a Marius (Michaelis 8). The bronze head in the Madagascar portrait is the "Arundel Homer" by virtue of the Earl's authority to confer that name upon it. Like the lyre of Amphion, the Earl Marshall's baton has the semi-magical power to call things into being—in the instance of the Madagascar portrait, an island colony, as Donne had said, quickly making "that, which was nothing, *all*."

Reinforcing the same connection between heraldic and artistic enterprise, the Earl Marshall's baton also appears in the earlier portrait of

Arundel with his collection of statuary, by Daniel Mytens (fig. 1), who also served the Earl as a purchasing agent of art in the Low Countries. The Mytens portrait of Arundel shows the Earl seated at the threshold of his sculpture gallery, while a companion portrait also by Mytens shows the Countess seated outside another long gallery in which paintings are displayed (fig. 2). The Countess sits composed, her own likeness echoing those of the other sitters whose portraits are depicted in the gallery. Juxtaposed with this image of contemporary art presided over by the Countess, Arundel takes a more active role as he draws our attention with his baton to the classical statues arrayed along the wall of the deep space opening behind him.

Within Mytens' painting of the Earl, the entrance to the gallery is set off by portals to either side of the door and by a high step at the bottom. So framed, this space can be read, ambiguously, as either the *painting* of a sculpture gallery or as an "actual" room in deep perspective. Mediated by the painting (as artwork and representational document), this fictive space is at once present as an architectural feature of Arundel House, and distant in time, an Albertian window opening into the classical past in which these statues first had their being. This *trompe l'oeil* effect is punctuated by the ambiguity of the baton. Its tip seems to indicate a detail on the surface of the painting-of-a-gallery, and yet to reach by some magical extension into the depth of the room itself so as to touch that same point in fact. At that point "in" the space of the gallery it "touches" the base of a statue resembling a Venus *pudica*, and by doing so it seems to animate the marble goddess. For she alone among the otherwise erect and impassive figures in her row seems to bestir herself in response to the Earl's gesture, seems to be just in the process of rousing herself to her full height through his influence. The collector's seeming power to restore the ancient world to life—like Vespucci waking "America" from her long torpor—is reflected as well in an anecdote told of Sir Francis Bacon. The great philosopher who had devoted his career to reinvigorating the diseased and vermiculate body of learning, "coming into the Earl of Arundel's Garden" in 1626, the last year of his life, and finding there "a great number of Ancient Statues of naked Men and Women, made a stand, and as astonish'd cryed out: *The Resurrection*" (Tenison 57).

This formal play of elements in the Mytens painting reflects an equally intriguing *trompe l'oeil* in the circumstances of the painting's composition. In fact, as David Howarth argues on the basis of other contemporary views and descriptions of the "decidedly old fashioned" gallery wing of Arundel House, the fine Italianate details of the room as depicted by Mytens are illusory, despite their meticulous rendering: "the barrel vault and the classical door cases and their consoles beneath, were no more real than that arched opening overlooking the Thames" (58–59). What is more, as Howarth goes on to show, the statues displayed in this imaginary room were not actually among those in Arundel's possession in 1616. Rather, in all likelihood, they represented a collection of sculpture he hoped to acquire in that year from Sir Dudley Carleton, the English ambassador in Venice. The Mytens portrait would then have been intended to serve as "part of [Arundel's] campaign to get Carleton to sell his statues," as Carleton might be more inclined to do if he were persuaded that in such elegant quarters as awaited them, they would "enjoy a setting worthy of their quality" (59).

Like the Madagascar portrait in relation to Arundel's prospective expedition to the island, this Mytens portrait does not so much represent its subject as implicate itself in its history. This sculpture gallery reveals the image of a collection in Arundel's mind, the vision of a potential reality no less alluring and no less fragile than the idea of a Madagascar colony in 1639. In Tara Hoag's phrase, both portraits engage us in a "visual paradox, a history of the future" (11), but a future in which, however imaginary, both participate in a direct and material way. As sales prospectuses their intention is to bring about in fact what they can only depict as fantasy. It is worth noting that the Earl Marshall's baton is itself a key part of the illusion conjured here: although the office had been a traditional honor in Arundel's family, in 1616 he would not come into sole possession of it for another five years. Possibly the image of his (would-be) success as a collector was also meant to further that ambition.

From the point of view of the later portrait of Arundel by Van Dyck, the Mytens sculpture gallery, like the island of Madagascar under the sway of Arundel's baton, may itself appear as a kind of colonial possession. A small subject population of marble figures is shipped in from afar like the native Americans put on display in the Jacobean court. Such figures, whether native Americans or Roman statues (and we should perhaps recall that in the iconography of the native American the two categories are often mixed) are objects of curiosity, fascination for the exotic, and potential profit; figures here authenticated, arrayed, and disciplined—put in good order—by the Earl Marshall's judicial authority as much as by his connoisseur's eye for the proper alignment of a sculpture gallery.

Even more clearly, the Madagascar portrait insists upon bolstering the colonial enterprise at hand with reminders of Arundel's prestige as a collector of art. In all versions of the painting, on a table to Arundel's left—partially concealed by the globe but emphasized for the viewer by their strategic proximity to the hand holding the baton—are "books and scroll of paper to represent, *pars pro toto*, Arundel's library." Behind them appear the bronze head of the Arundel Homer, mentioned above as lending an epic cast to the impending voyage, "and a marble head, probably restored as Apollo." The purpose of the display, as this commentator goes on to conclude, is to "make evident the magnanimity of the Madagascar scheme. Learning and the arts will assist in the pursuit of the project but their advancement also will reflect the nobility in the name of which the Arundels propose to exercise the rule of Madagascar" (Aldrich, I caption to his fig. 13). In fact, these heads rest here at the half-way point of their own cultural trade route. Under Arundel's heraldic aegis, objects of art imported from abroad will be accorded their proper place in the domestic order of things. In turn the civilizing benefits incorporated and commemorated in the heraldic art will be exported to Madagascar.

The link between colonial and artistic acquisition is strengthened in the copy of the Madagascar portrait at Knole (fig. 4) by the presence of a figure in the background—his hand resting on Homer's head, in a visual echo of Arundel's hand resting on the globe of the world—a figure who, as I have noted at the beginning, may be either William Petty or Francis Junius. It seems beside the point to try to resolve this disputed identification. It is telling that a plausible case may be made for either man, for in Arundel's enterprises the purchasing agent and the classical scholar figured as the two sides of the same coin.

In appearance, this mysterious figure bears little resemblance to Junius as he was painted by Van Dyck himself only a year later, in a portrait of 1640 now in the Bodleian (fig. 7). Strengthening the claim for Petty is the fact that this confidante of Arundel had just died in September, 1639. There is some evidence that in 1637 Arundel planned to set aside a room for "Designes" at Arundel House that would be furnished with both a portrait and a marble bust of his trusted agent, and that it was Petty who encouraged Junius to undertake his scholarly researches into the history of art (Springell 194–95). It is not certain how the bronze head long known as the "Arundel Homer" and represented in the Madagascar portrait came into the Earl's possession, but Petty may have had a hand in this important acquisition as in so many others on Arundel's behalf (Ashmolean 62). As Howarth argues, Petty's inclusion in at least one version of the Madagascar portrait would be an appropriate commemoration. Petty's energy and shrewdness had more than anything else made possible the Arundel collections as, for a period of fifteen years before his death, he had scoured Italy, Greece, and Asia Minor on the commission of his patron, acquiring marbles, old manuscripts and a host of other antiquities, often in competition with agents dispatched by Buckingham to the same territories. Howarth also notices the "abundance of paper" in the portrait. This, he suggests, is entirely appropriate for Petty, in that "the whole collection had been built on a mountain of paper—upon those hundreds of letters which passed between Arundel and Petty, all but a handful of which have vanished" (169).

Insofar as the head of the "Arundel Homer" gives the art of collecting itself a kind of epic scope, Petty would seem to fit the role of a latter-day Odysseus better than the retiring and scholarly Junius. Correspondence from the 1620s from Sir Thomas Roe, then ambassador to Constantinople, to Buckingham and Arundel

> gives a vivid picture of Petty's energy and determination; it recounts also the hardship and great risk which Petty had to undergo in his activities, his fearlessness and his utter disregard of severe personal danger. For the purpose of collecting classical antiquities he also visited the mainland of Greece and the Greek islands, and in 1625, while returning from a successful visit to Samos, he suffered shipwreck near the coast of Asia Minor, lost all the objects he had collected at the expense of great labour and personal privation and was furthermore in grave danger of losing his life. As he lost the ambassador's letters of introduction and other identity papers on that occasion, he was promptly arrested by the Turkish authorities as a spy and only freed after Roe's intervention. (Springell 196–97)

Undaunted, Petty bought up another shipload which, delivered to England, became the basis for Selden's *Marmora Arundeliana* (1628). Selden's praise for Petty's "ardent and incomparable devotion to the glory of old Greek art" (qtd. Hervey 280) would surely justify his place in any painting commissioned by the Earl in which that art was so prominently displayed.

Yet other scholars, including Sir Oliver Millar, still think the figure in the upper right corner of the Knole version is Junius, and this traditional identification has its own compelling logic. Junius had been the Earl's librarian since 1621, the year Arundel had been created Earl Marshall, and also the year in which, perhaps not coincidentally, Arundel had "embarked on a great scheme to enlarge his already considerable and for English circumstances, altogether astonishing collection of antiquities" (Aldrich I xxxvii). Van Dyck had consulted Junius at least once before the Madagascar portrait, in 1636, about an appropriate inscription for a portrait of Sir Kenelm Digby. The artist was then preparing to publish a series of engraved portraits of famous contemporaries known as the *Iconography*, a collection of modern worthies to match his patron's collection of antiquities. Digby was to have a place of honor in this pantheon, and no one was better qualified than Junius to supply an apt classical tag. One Van Dyck scholar is convinced that the scheme of the Madagascar portrait was drawn up by Arundel with Junius's help (Brown 209). Junius's inclusion in the Knole version of the portrait would then be an appropriate acknowledgment of all these services, both to the patron and the painter.

Junius had also provided important logistical support for Arundel's collecting campaign. Among his other philological and historical projects—and as part of the same research that would lead to *The Painting of the Ancients*—he had worked for years to compile an encyclopedic *Catalogus* of antiquities. This was to be a comprehensive alphabetical list of ancient painters, sculptors, and other artisans from Aaron (who made the Golden Calf) to Zosimus, noted in a Roman inscription as surpassing all others "in the art of engraving Clodian silverware" (Aldrich II, 424). For each name, the catalogue entry lists, and where possible describes, the works attributed to the same artist in the classical sources. It also contains entries for works by anonymous artists, and such generic entries as "Alexandrian tapestries" and "Cumaean dishes," the latter a particularly luxurious kind of red earthenware mentioned in Pliny and Martial. The *Catalogus* was not published until 1694, long after Junius's death. Completed by 1628, however, it was arguably intended to serve a very practical purpose, allowing Arundel—or his agents, if they were to carry manuscript copies of it into the field—to tell whether a piece offered for sale matched the classical accounts, and so was more or less likely to be what it was represented to be by the seller. We know from his correspondence that Junius was keen on seeing all his other books through the press. The fact that the *Catalogus* was *not* published may in itself suggest an interest in keeping so valuable a reference guide to the antiquities market out of the hands of the competition.

In this respect, Junius's authority as an arbiter of the authentic in the realm of art doubles that of the Earl Marshall in the realm of heraldry. But their imaginative correspondence, as the Madagascar portrait implies, runs deeper still. Junius's scholarship, in *The Painting of the Ancients* as well as in the *Catalogus*, has the power to recover—for the mind's eye at least—a wealth of visual riches unseen for millennia but now excavated from their literary repositories. Like the idea of Madagascar in Arundel's mind, the far-removed realm of ancient art appears, in Junius's phrase, as a "conceived presence" in the author's book. Junius's epic voyages in the seas of classical learning—if less thrilling than Petty's actual shipwrecks—yield a near-exhaustive survey of all references to the visual arts in the literature of the Greeks and Romans, and so open up the world of antiquity. Arundel's agents follow the Homeric routes to return from the shores of Ilium with treasures that will now accrue to the glory of Britain. It is to Arundel, writes Henry Peacham in 1634, in the second edition of *The Compleat Gentleman*, that "this angle of the world oweth the first sight of Greeke and Romane Statues, with whose admired presence he began to honour the Gardens and Galleries of Arundel-House about twentie yeeres agoe, and hath ever since continued to transplant old Greece into England." Peacham records the fact that the King personally examined these treasures on a visit to Arundel House in 1629 and was inspired to build a collection of his own. Indeed, so great became the "Royall liking of ancient statues," that Charles caused "a whole army of old forraine Emperors, Capitaines, and Senators all at once to land on his coasts, to come and doe him homage, and attend him in his palaces of St James and Sommerset House" (107–108). In their parallel contributions to this cultural work, Junius offers the model of the *vita contemplativa* to set against Petty's *vita activa*, the scholar and the hero whose joint efforts assist in the return of emperors, captains and senators to Britain, now not as conquerors but as the conquered.

The transplantation of the past from "old" Greece and Rome into England offers, in turn, a precedent and a model for the future cultivation of Madagascar, the site of a new colony transplanted from England. In this cultural commerce, what Arundel takes from the peripheral world in art and antiquities, he will refund to Madagascar in the civilizing influence of which these very objects are the sign. The coincidence of the word "transplant" in Peacham's account of the importation of classical culture and in the common currency of colonial discourse is revealing. "Transplantation" has its literal sense in the movement of people to new places where they become "planters," and in the transplantaton of food grains (and pathogens) from the old world to the new and back again. It also implies a deeper continuity between the two modes of *translatio imperii*: the movement of empire from its "antique springs" (Jonson's phrase for the sources of his teacher Camden's learning) in the remains of Greece and Rome to England, where it will spring anew in the hands of such expert cultivators as Arundel, and from which it will be transplanted again to fresh seedbeds in far-off island possessions.Such colonial tranplantation, it is important to note, figures doubly as the cultivation of a new world and the re-cultivation of the old, the renovation of the broadly eastern world of antiquity long since fallen into ruin. In *The Anatomy of Melancholy* (1621) Burton had asked rhetorically, "[W]hy is that fruitful Palestine, noble Greece, Egypt, Asia Minor, so much decayed, and (mere carcasses now) fallen from that they were?" (74). The answer was not hard to find. It was not that the land was any less fertile, but that the inhabitants have long neglected their responsibility for its tillage:

> The ground is the same, but the government is altered, the people are grown

> slothful, idle, their good husbandry, policy, and industry is decayed. The soil is not tired nor exhausted, as Columella well informed Sylvinus, but barren through our own laziness, &c.... If any man from Mount Taygetus should view the country round about, and see so many delicate and brave cities built with such cost and exquisite cunning, so neatly set out in Peloponnesus, he should perceive them now ruinous and overthrown, burnt, waste, desolate, and laid level with the ground. ...To shut up all in brief, where good government is, prudent and wise Princes, there all things thrive and prosper, peace and happiness is in that land: where it is otherwise, all things are ugly to behold, incult, barbarous, uncivil, a Paradise is turned to a wilderness. (74–75)

The solution is to understand that civility and good government are the fruits of a long historical march of colonization: "This Island [that is, Britain] in a short time, by that prudent policy of the Romans, was brought from barbarism; see but what Caesar reports of us, and Tacitus of those old Germans; they were once as uncivil as they in Virginia, yet by planting of colonies and good laws, they became, from barbarous outlaws, to bc full of rich and populous cities, as now they are, and most flourishing kingdoms." The lesson for the future is clear: "Even so might Virginia, and those wild Irish, have been civilized long since, if that order had been heretofore taken, which now begins of planting colonies" (71). The seeds carried into Britain by the Romans will be replanted in the barren but receptive soil of Britain's colonies, restoring wildernesses to paradises. In Van Dyck's portrait the emblems of Arundel's success as a collector—the scrolls, the head of Homer, the bust of Apollo, the figure of Junius (or Petty) clustered around the globe—all augur the success of the Earl Marshall's impending colonial expedition to the Indian Ocean and support his implied warrant to undertake such a voyage. The Arundel marbles, having literally been dug out of the ground like dormant seeds and figuratively resuscitated by Arundel's art, will now be disseminated in their civilizing virtue to other climes. Such enterprises will, in Burton's legal phrase, bring the "barbarous outlaw" under the sway of the law. Old foreign emperors will come to do homage in the palaces of the new ruler, to confer upon him the legitimacy that will now re-establish and extend the *imperium* they have forsaken. But, as befits a medical treatise on the causes and remedies of melancholy, the colonial mission also takes on a wonderful therapeutic power, restoring life to the "mere carcasses" of the ancient world. Travel itself, Burton advises, "must needs refresh and give content to a melancholy dull spirit" (444).

The immediate effect of an expedition to Madagascar may be to offer a cure for Arundel's melancholy. Yet in its power to act at a distance on the decayed and barren lands it will restore to cultural health, colonization works much like those controversial therapies that (as we shall see in chapter 4) filled the pages of medical polemics in the 1630s, the "Powder of Sympathy" and the "Weapons-Salve."

In the light of such cultural transplantation we can look again at the Van Dyck portrait of the Earl and his grandson (fig. 5) by way of an earlier portrait by Van Dyck, done at Rome and dating from 1622–3, of George Gage (fig. 8). Gage is an obscure figure, apparently involved at once in the politics of religious and artistic intrigue. Sir Dudley Carleton, James's ambassador to Venice, reports during the winter of 1613–14 that Arundel and the Countess have turned up in Rome despite official prohibitions on travel by English tourists to that sinkhole of papist corruption. He would not have believed it if he had not "spoken wth some who had seen them there," but Carleton's qualms are partly allayed in that he has heard "of no English who did much resort unto them but Toby Mathew and George Gage, neither of any course they took for other purposes than the satisfying of curiosity" (qtd. Hervey 83–84). Carleton's report implies that, however uneventful the contact may have been, resorting to the likes of Gage is not to the Arundels' credit. Gage and Mathew both took holy orders from Cardinal Bellarmine at Rome later that year, in May, 1614 (*DNB*). In the 1620s Gage acted as an intermediary in Rome on behalf of James during the protracted and fruitless negotiation to secure a papal dispensation for Prince Charles to marry the Spanish Infanta—the ill-fated "Spanish match." Gage's name appears, finally, among those priests and recusants arrested for their subversive activities in England between 1640–1651. Quite possibly he died in prison.

Gage played the same ambidextrous mediating role as a facilitator in the art and antiquities trade, becoming, in the 1630s, a successful rival of Thomas Roe and Arundel's invaluable William Petty as "one of Charles I's most effective agents in the building up of his great collection" (Brown 74). Van Dyck portrays him in this very role, leaning casually, even with a certain insouciance, on a ledge on which his family arms are carved as a means of identifying the sitter as Gage. In contrast with his relaxed pose, his face is bright with a watchful alertness as he attends to the man to his left proffering a statuette identified by Howarth as "a reduced version of the *Aphrodite*, now one of the Arundel marbles in the Ashmolean Museum" (158). This man is furtive, insistent, suspicious—in Howarth's words, "combative and tense as a greyhound as he leans forward to press a sale" (158). Negotiations have begun but the game is young, and there is a whiff of danger. The scene has the air of a chance encounter, but perhaps that is just the impression intended to be conveyed by Gage's pose. Christopher Brown observes that Gage "registers interest, but, like a skillful poker player, is careful not to appear too enthusiastic" (76).

These descriptions catch the mood of the art market depicted here, but not Van Dyck's complex portrayal of Gage's pivotal role in a larger cultural drama. Gage's head and that of the dealer are the most prominent in the painting. Both are in the foreground, strongly lit, and each is the object of the other's assessing gaze. These two are, however, part of a suite of four heads clustered in the upper right of the painting, including the two partly shadowed in the background: that of the statuette, and that of a black servant (as he appears to be) mirroring the dealer's gesture of pointing to the marble with one hand while (perhaps) supporting its weight with the other (hidden behind the sculpture). The picture is, in fact, a carefully composed roundelay of hands as well as heads. One of its starkest visual contrasts is that between the strong, purposeful gesture of the black man's finger indicating the object for sale, and the very pale, very thin and fragile-looking hands of George Gage, the left one hanging limply off the shelf on which he supports his arm. A line running through these two carefully opposed hands, the servant's dark right hand and Gage's strangely bloodless left hand, defines one major diagonal controlling the design of the painting, just as a line connecting Gage's eyes with the broker's defines another. The former diagonal continues up to the right corner of the painting, to the head of the marble statue whose stony hue more closely resembles the pallor of Gage's hand than does the warm flesh tone of Gage's own face, even as the hand's flaccid droop forms a contrast with the rigidity of the marble.

Formal similarities and contrasts of this kind could be multiplied. For example, while the rough and open heartiness of the servant's expression acts as a foil to the polished sophistication of Gage's, and the dealer and his servant are professionally allied against Gage in the transaction under way, nevertheless Gage and the servant—their heads tilted toward one another in opposition to the dealer's—also share a sense of mutual *bon-homie* completely lacking in the dealer's nearly ferocious glare. If we focus on the interrelationship of the three human heads, the rather swarthy dealer mediates between the servant and Gage in the color of their complexion, while Gage mediates between the servant and the dealer not only positionally in space (he is "between" them in the paintings recession in depth, just as the servant is between the other two on the surface of the canvas), but in a look that combines something of the servant's good humor with something of the dealer's intense concentration. The marble statuette, the inanimate if crucial focus of the implied narrative (the picture is "about" her, about the desire to possess her, to purchase her just as the black servant was presumably purchased in his turn by the man who now offers the sculpture for sale) nonetheless takes on something of a human aspect and animation in this company. She seems to twist her body away from the probing finger of the servant, seems to want to force herself not to look at this scene of her own merchandising.

These many small notations point beyond the formal sophistication of Van Dyck's style. Together they create an image not only of this particular transaction but an implied history of antiquities dealing in which the black servant, relegated to the background of the painting, nonetheless figures prominently. What the painting shows in this (dimly allegorical) light is the handing-over of the goddess from the dark man whose origins lie on the geographical periphery whence she herself comes, to the middle man who will place her in the hands of Gage—who will, in turn, give her to those for whom he acts as agent. It is an image of a transmission as well as a transaction, of the removal of the old gods to their new habitation. The goddess is the object that visually connects the exotic background of the painting denizened by the black servant with the European foreground. She has covered the distance and traversed the time separating her world from this present place and moment.

In this interchange, the other sculptural motif in the painting, Gage's coat of arms at the bottom right (balancing the statuette on the top right) assumes a significance greater than as a clue to the identity of the sitter.

In a market where the goddess offered for sale may or may not be genuine, the arms certify Gage's authenticity. As he supports himself on the ledge on which they are carved, they provide him with a firm genealogical as well as visual basis. As himself a visual echo of the statuette in the painting (their heads and torsos are turned in the same direction), resting on his own foundation, Gage almost seems to pose himself as a work of art (in the same measure as the goddess almost seems to come to life). Furthermore, insofar as the ram's head, the crest of the Gage family arms, refigures the blunt animal strength of the black servant—we recall Iago's taunting characterization of Othello as the "black ram"—it declares that Gage is the legitimate heir of the ancient realm he represents, and thus the legitimate owner of its artifacts. In its fullest resonance the painting is not only about buying a statue but insuring and continuing an historical order in which the buyer is honored in and by that very act.

The 1635 Van Dyck portrait of Arundel and his grandson, for all its obvious differences from that of Gage, depicts the Earl in a similar mediating role once the circumstances of the painting are taken into account. Howarth suggests with some plausibility that the two figures represented are based on a fragment of funerary sculpture known to have been in the Earl's collection of marbles, a bas relief showing an adult and a child in the same general pose as that in the Van Dyck double portrait (161). If he is right about the sculptural context of this image, we may think of it as coming to be by a kind of metamorphosis from its stony origin. In effect it comes to life, just as the statue of Venus in the Mytens painting of the Earl's gallery seems to be waking from its frozen sleep at the touch of Arundel's staff—the same staff as he holds in this portrait and, we recall, in the Madagascar portrait, signifying his genealogical authority as a herald, the Earl Marshall's power to "create." What had appeared on an ancient sarcophagus as the image of death is rejuvenated, as much in the rich colors of Van Dyck's art as in its focus on the grand-child and in the promise for the future that he represents under Arundel's tutelage and protection. Furthermore, as Howarth also notes, Arundel writes to William Petty in 1636 that he is sending him this same painting, "a Picture of my owne and my little Tom bye me," with the "desire it may be done at Florence in marble *Basso relievo*, to try a yonge Sculptor there who is said to be *valente Huomo* (Hervey 391). The identity of the young sculptor can only be guessed at, and this would not be the only painting sent abroad to serve as a sculptor's model—one thinks of the more famous "triple head" of Charles I painted by Van Dyck in 1635 for the studio of Bernini. Nonetheless Arundel's intention in this case is uniquely fascinating, for to commit his image to the hand of the young Florentine sculptor who would (re)create it as a marble *"Basso relievo"* would be to complete the circle by returning it to stone—from ancient bas relief, to the portrait taken from the life, and then, through the artistry of the young Florentine sculptor, back to the form reminiscent of its funerary origin.

Arundel and his little Tom, as painted by Van Dyck, thus stand at the center of a complex mediation between the old world and the new. Playing a role in its way like that of Van Dyck's image of the goddess in the Gage portrait, they connect an ancient work of art with its modern replication, and the site from which that fragment of sculpture was broken off with the English collection in which it has found its place. They connect a long-dead sculptor with a "yonge" one now in Florence who, thanks to Arundel, will take instruction from that same ancient master—just as, within the painting, young Tom, holding a paper, looks up (and back) to his grandfather Thomas with a pupil's mixture of respect and fear toward a stern teacher. The painting's image of the transmission of learning and authority from one generation to the next is writ large in the more sweeping act of cultural transmission in which it implicated by Arundel's gesture of returning it to the Mediterranean world. What came as a funerary image is now renovated by an art that will make the picture speak across the ages to the new sculptor who will reclaim it.The translation of the image from stone to pigment to stone is the formal product of a cultural *translatio* in time and space, from the imperium of antiquity to modern England and back again to the same place by the authority of Arundel.

One question, otherwise trivial perhaps, suggests itself in this context. If the theme so powerfully articulated in this painting is the passage of authority from one generation to the next—the bond of paternal and filial obligation by which the dead past is re-collected and handed down to the "yonge"—then we may ask: where is the father who should stand between the Thomas and Tom, the grandfather and the grandson? How are we to account for the gap concealed, as it were by the very proximity of the two figures? The history of the painting itself lends a certain plausibility to this concern, however speculative it may seem, since at Newstead Abbey where the picture hung in the last century it was mistakenly described as a portrait of the Earl and his *son*. In a sonnet written on this painting, Matthew Arnold sees Arundel as the "stern, mailed father" remorseful (as the poet imagines) for having "struck, in heat" his "little fair-haired son" ("A Picture at Newstead," Allot 481–82).

It may be, of course, that Arundel simply wanted himself painted with the grandchild who would carry on his Christian name, and for whom he had a special fondness. The child's father, Arundel's second son and heir Henry Frederick, Lord Maltravers, sat separately for Van Dyck, who painted him in armor much like Arundel's in this portrait (Hervey pl. XV, facing p. 334). There was a son named Thomas, Arundel's third-born, who died as a child, as did the fourth of his four sons, Gilbert. Indeed, with the death of his first-born son James in 1623, at the age of sixteen, Henry Frederick became the sole survivor among Arundel's progeny. By his absence from this portrait, Maltravers stands (out) for the missing generation of his brothers, while "yonge Tom" stands (in) for the his uncle and Arundel's son, the dead child Thomas—a kind of commemoration for which the funerary history of the image is entirely appropriate, and deeply evocative of Arundel's loss.

The absent father brings to mind—and may have brought to mind for the Earl—Arundel's own father Philip, imprisoned for most of Arundel's childhood and dead in the Tower when Arundel was ten, about the same age as little Tom in this painting. In Van Dyck's portrait, Arundel also "stands in" for his own lost father, as well as for the father of his grandson. Having, as it were, revived this child from his cold marble image on an antique sarcophagus, the painting enacts the double purpose of restoring the generation of the dead son Thomas in his namesake, while securing at least the lively image of this child (as Arundel protectively places a hand on the boy's shoulder) from their sad fate. In the lineage of his own family as in the longer cultural lineage running through the painting, Arundel (the "father of virtu in England") connects dead sons with living ones: ultimately, the dead child on the sarcophagus with the young sculptor in Florence, in whom Arundel takes a necessarily distant but warmly paternal interest.

What are the implications of the convergences we have been tracing by means of the Van Dyck portraits and their ancillary texts? One is a reminder that a book like Junius's *Painting of the Ancients*—long canonical in the history of art scholarship as the first comprehensive survey of classical objects, practices and commentaries, as reflected in the literary archive—nonetheless should be understood first of all as the product of its own historical moment. The most influential scholarly work to come out of the Arundel circle, it would remain the standard source on classical art until the time of Winckelmann, and it was still sufficiently prestigious in the later 18th century for Lessing to challenge its authority in the *Laocoön* as enmeshed in an untheoretical confusion of poetry and painting. In this tradition we tend to think of Junius—not mistakenly, but detached from any particular circumstances—as having made a founding contribution to the to the history of aesthetic theory. However, as we have seen, in the context of Arundel's overlapping projects of the 1630s, Junius's scholarship has its more complex rationale as well as its more immediate practical uses.

Disciplinary histories tend to absorb and canonize their founding works by claiming for them, explicitly or in effect, a timeless pertinence that conceals the conditions of their origin. A closer look at the Caroline art market in which Junius plays a key role reveals the liaison of dealers, collectors, and art historians. The discipline of art history, creating itself in the late Renaissance by the appropriation of a field of study within the larger domain of classical scholarship, is inseparable from the appropriation of the artworks it authenticates, classifies, and evaluates. These connections may prompt us to speak of a colonization of art, a venture in which Junius's scholarship, Van Dyck's portraiture and the farflung enterprises of Arundel and his transnational antiquities brokers are joined. Conversely, we may also speak of an art of colonization, of colonization as an *ars*—a phrase that describes the Van Dyck painting in a literal sense, as well as the Earl's larger visionary and commercial designs on Madagascar. On the evidence of the Madagascar portrait, the founding discourse of colonialism, as it interweaves such diverse strands as heraldry, antiquities, classical scholarship, and painting itself, is both subtler and more diverse in Arundel's world than we may be led to suppose if we look at its history from too narrowly a political or economic point of view.

Those of us accustomed to working primarily with the evidence of visual and literary culture, especially when our view of the English Renaissance has tended to be refracted through the prism of our latterday "post-colonial" assumptions, need to take into account the nominalist position argued forcefully and with near unanimity by historians of English expansionism in the sixteenth and earlier seventeenth centuries. For the English, as late as Arundel's chimerical colony in Madagascar, and indeed well past mid century, the British "empire" (with the significant exception of its dominion over Ireland) existed largely in the imagination of the visionary. According to John Appleby, when John Dee used (perhaps coined) the phrase "British Impire" in the 1570s to "justify England's claim to the North Atlantic," his case was based on the "mythical conquests of King Arthur and Prince Madoc, the latter allegedly the first discoverer of North American in the twelfth century" (62). During the Protectorate Cromwell conceived the "Western Design" of 1654–55, a plan to export the Revolution of the Saints to the new world, which fizzled in a "disastrous attempt to seize Hispaniola as a base for a subsequent invasion of the Spanish-American mainland" (Pagden 35).

Even these instances in which the word, if not the reality, of an "imperial" impulse referred to the larger world were exceptional. Normally, phrases like "great Brittaines imperial crowne" or "the Empire of Great Britaine" referred, after 1603, to the united kingdoms of England, Scotland, and Ireland, and the principality of Wales. Carrying "no neccessary expansionist associations," Britain's imperial status implied just the opposite: her independence from foreign control, her isolation and self-sufficiency, rather than any ambition on her part toward foreign dominion (Canny 1). David Armitage argues that not until after the Restoration

> did the British Empire come to include the territorial settlements of North America and the Caribbean or the factories of Africa and Asia; even then it was couched in the form of "the British Empire *in* America" or "the British Empire *of* America," implying the territory over which the authority of the monarchy was exercised rather than a unitary political body.... That sense of the British

> Empire seems only to have appeared in the second quarter of the eighteenth century. (113)

Until the 1630s and 1640s, the history of British expansionist amibitions overseas was still very largely a history of failure, punctuated by such "violent and humiliating failures" as those in "North and South America, embodied in the lost colony of Roanoke and the repeated debacles of plantation efforts in the region of the Amazon" (Games 2). Even then, at the moment of its emergence, this "empire" consisted of privateering expeditions, trading posts, more or less speculative ventures promoted by the proliferating number of companies (East India, Virginia, Bermuda, Levant, Muscovy, Massachusetts Bay, New England), the crown, and individual entrepreneurs like Arundel. Indeed, as an emblem of these early years, the collapse of the Earl's Madagascar scheme makes it entirely typical of the haphazard and precarious chararacter of English colonialism—not so much an "empire" in any later sense of the word, as a "motley assortment of competing interests," as yet lacking any "coherence in direction or ideology" (Games 3).

My intention in the case of Arundel's Madagascar has been to explore the early sources of such coherence in a work of art. The Van Dyck portrait does not reflect pre-existent reasons of state or economic policies from which the more overt features of that coherence would ultimately take shape. Instead it creates a matrix for the protocolonial imagination, engendering the stuff that Arundel's dreams were made on. In this, of course, it is not unique. Images of sea monsters, Homeric Amazons, Ovidian witches, Antipodeans, and men whose heads do grow beneath their shoulders populated the margins of the known world, hovering somewhere between fiction and reality, and fleshing out a geography of the unknown by which not even Raphael Hythloday's Utopians were completely implausible. Earlier explorations had always been guided to a large extent by the light of the imagination. In the 1570s John Davis and Martin Frobisher searched the frozen bays and inlets of the Canadian north for what they were sure must be there: a northwest passage as a counterpart to the Strait of Magellan. Similarly, the belief in the existence of a northeast passage to match the Cape of Good Hope in the south led Willoughby and Chancellor on a fruitless quest around the

North Cape of Norway—which providentially sat along the same line of latitude in the north as the horn of Africa in the south—into the Barents Sea (Keay 6–9). Such expectations were based on a sense of creative design too durable to be erased even by the mounting, and painful, evidence of its fictiveness: symmetry required that the northern and southern hemispheres reflect one another. That there is a "north" America and "south" America only confirms the rationale by which it had been held since Pliny that there was a similarly correspondent relation between the land and the sea ("horses" in both), and by which it must now be assumed that the two northern passages must exist as the reflection of their southern counterpart. Just as these aesthetic assumptions set the actual course of English navigation, Van Dyck's portrait, as well as other works such as Davenant's "Madagascar," create the kind of colonial fiction that would then be available for the representation, and misrepresentation, of colonial realities once the ships set sail in earnest (See Appendix 1). Even in our own time, Aimé Césaire's rewriting of *The Tempest* as a means of understanding the postcolonial experience of the Caribbean testifies to the persistent force of such shaping fantasies. Arundel's arts combine those of the herald, the collector of antiquities, and the patron of painters and scholars. Those arts are not peripheral to Arundel's role as the would-be creator of a colonial plantation, or to the creation of an early modern colonial ideology. Rather, they define it.

2. Franciscus Junius and *The Painting of the Ancients*: The Labors of Isis

> See *Prudentius* in the passion of *Cassianus* the Schoolmaster, who was by his own school-boyes, the tyrant forcing them thereunto, prickt to death with the sharpe points of their writing bodkins.
>
> *The Painting of the Ancients* (155)

As this chapter and the next will be concerned with the commemorative powers of art, art collecting, and writing about art, it seems fitting to begin with this brief memorial of the death of Cassianus. Junius is here describing a lost painting of the Saint's unusual martyrdom, preserved only in the writings of Prudentius, and recollected by Arundel's librarian as evidence that the "The monuments of Martyrs were adorned with paintings, setting forth all the circumstances of the butcherlike crueltie used against the Saints of God" (155). The painting of Cassianus "prickt to death," a warning to all classroom teachers, may also serve as the emblem of Junius's project in *The Painting of the Ancients*. It is, in fact, a blind emblem: there is no extant painting of Cassianus to be seen. Like the hundreds, if not thousands, of other pictures and statues chronicled in the literature of antiquity—including the works of such fabled masters as Apelles, Praxiteles, or Protogenes—this "Passion of Cassianus" can only be imagined. We would surely have seen the schoolmaster resolved in his suffering, and the Roman soldiers with drawn swords enforcing the tyrant's wrath. Would the school boys have been weeping in compassion for their fallen instructor, or perhaps shown (some of the more rambunctious of them) as getting into the spirit of the thing?

Where it cannot supply a picture, Junius's example implies a condensed historical narrative of bereavement and recovery. The loss of Cassianus, and then the loss of the image that adorned his monument, is restored, if only partially: first through the account of his martyrdom in the Latin poetry of Prudentius (himself an authority indispensable to Renaissance schoolmasters for his *Psychomachia*), and now through Junius's citation of Prudentius's text. The victim of his students' "writing bodkins," Cassianus owes both his death and the survival of his saintly reputation to the "sharpe pointes" of his followers' pens. This irony joins the two halves of Junius's chiastic narrative: the *instrumenta passionis* of the schoolmaster's martyrdom will become, in time, the only means of his commemoration, as well as the only commemoration of a dead visual tradition.

In what follows, I will want to argue that the importance of Junius's work in resurrecting this tradition goes beyond the particular theoretical positions he synthesizes, and beyond the usefulness of his book as a thesaurus of classical passages on the visual arts. Both these aspects of his influence have been treated in the few special studies devoted to him, as well as in the introduction and annotations to the California edition of *The Painting of the Ancients*, published in 1991. My own procedure in starting with an image rather than an argument is intended to get at a different, and as I shall argue, even more compelling part of the book's importance as a document in the early modern history of visual culture: its imaginative vitality. Junius's great achievement in defining the field of classical art was to have imagined a thing never seen, and then to have imagined how it might be repossessed. To read Junius's treatise as a work *of*, as well as *about*, the imagination is to regard it as I believe he himself would wish us to do. For it is, as Junius claims in the Argument to the first book, the "delight stirred up by our imagination" that emboldens us "undertake greater matters" (2). *The Painting of the Ancients*, we know, was read in its own time with pleasure as well as profit by Arundel, Van Dyck, and Rubens, who sent Junius a congratulatory letter on its publication. In exploring its cultural importance then and now, I try to recover something of the delight to be found in a work that, in the hands of modern scholars, has tended less to be given a sympathetic reading than strip-mined for its erudition.

Of all the figures in the Arundel circle, Junius is perhaps the most prolific and the least known today, except to specialists in the fields of Germanic philology. Francis, or Franciscus, Junius the Younger was born in 1589 in Heidelberg. His father, the distinguished biblical scholar Franciscus Junius the Elder (or François Du Jon, in his native Bourges), soon moved the family to Leiden, where he served as professor of theology. With the death of the elder Junius in 1602, the son grew close to his uncle, the classicist and theologian Gerardus Vossius (Gerhard Johann Voss). Vossius was director of the theological college at Leiden, then professor of rhetoric, chronology, and Greek, and finally professor of history at the new Athenaeum in Amsterdam, a post he held until his death in 1649. (In 1629, with his nephew in London, Vossius strengthened the family's English ties by accepting Archbishop Laud's offer of a prebend without residence in Canterbury cathedral).

After taking his degree in theology Junius became pastor at Hillgondsberg in 1617. By the end of 1621, however, he is writing to Vossius from London (12/11/1621: BM Harley MS 7012, fol. 24), beginning a steady correspondence that would continue throughout the twenty years of Junius's sojourn in England. He had arrived over the summer. The Earl of Arundel, possibly on the recommendation of Lancelot Andrewes, wanted to engage him. By May, 1622 it has been decided that Junius will tutor Arundel's ten-year-old son William, dividing his time between the house of Samuel Harsnett, Bishop of Norwich, with whom the boy has been living for the past two years, and Arundel House in London, where he will tend to the Earl's library. In this letter, Junius asks his uncle to ship over a number of his books, presumably for use with his young pupil (5/31/1622 to Vossius: Bod. MS Rawl. Lett. 79, fol. 58).

That one of the books requested by the new school master was a volume of poems by Hugo Grotius may offer a clue to Junius's rather sudden removal to England. Vossius and Grotius, Arminians both, had long been friends. Vossius's *Historia Pelagiana* (1618) was attacked by orthodox Calvinists as reeking of Arminianism, but it would have nurtured the budding scholar in Junius by treating the Pelagian controversy from an historical point of view—just as Grotius's researches into the historical and biblical underpinnings of international relations would, in 1625, result in the publication of his *Concerning the Law of War and Peace*. In May, 1621, before embarking for England, Junius wrote to his sister Johanna that he had heard the report of Grotius's marvelous escape from his confinement in Castle Loewesteyn: the illustrious prisoner had been secreted out, concealed in a bookcase. Junius goes on to say that he went to Paris to see the great jurist in person, and that he talked with Grotius about his own reasons for leaving Holland. It is possible that the lure of employment in England was accompanied by the fear of religious persecution at home (5/5/1621: Bod. MS Rawl Lett. 79, fol. 60). Junius himself apparently felt no very strong sacred calling, but his ultimately 'Arminian' faith in the perfectibility of the creative spirit by the "grace" of art would have been more warmly received in Arundel House than in his Calvinist homeland.

After twenty years with Arundel, Junius returned to the Netherlands. The English civil war had broken Arundel's spirit as well as his already weakened health. The Arundel circle was broken, too. The Earl and the Countess were about to go into their own final (and separate) exiles on the continent, he to Padua where he died in 1646, she to Amsterdam. Junius was in England again for a time in 1648, apparently to represent the interests of the Countess in a legal imbroglio over the disposition of that part of the Earl's collection of paintings and antiquities remaining in Arundel House (see Aldrich, I, xlii and Hervey, 471–2). Back in Leiden, but soon finding that city "pitiefully decaied" and a "most sicklie desolate place," in the end the octogenarian scholar returned to England for good, in 1674, to pursue his Anglo-Saxon studies. He moved to Oxford in 1676 to be near his former pupil Thomas Marshall, now Rector of Lincoln College but formerly a preacher at Dort, where he and Junius had collaborated in the publication of *Observationes in Evangeliorum Versiones perantiques duas, Gothicas scil. et Anglo-Saxonicas* in 1665.

One of Junius's hopes during his ninth decade was to revise his work on ancient painting. As he had written to John Cotton in 1670 (1/30?1670: Bod., MS Smith 25, fol. 37):

> I intend shortly, by the assistance of our gracious God to send my *Pictura veterum* to the presse again, much altered and enlarged; beeing about to praemitte before it a new work, entituled *Catalogus artificum*, wherein a man may finde Alphabetically sett downe the lifes of all the most famous painters, statuaries, sculptors, carvers &c. that ever I found mentioned in Greek or Latin classike auctors. But although I have great reason to hasten the printing what I can, as beeing yesterday entred into my fourscoreth year, yet shall I for all that

> never cease (God maintaining the strength of my outward, and upholding the vigour of my inward parts) to serve the publike and you, by whose treasure of antiquities my Saxon studies have bene much promoted.

This edition of Junius's Latin text, however, would be brought out only posthumously, in 1694, in Rotterdam, by the classical scholar Johann Georg Graevius. The "new work" to which Junius refers, the encyclopedic *Catalogus* of ancient artists published here for the first time, was in fact a project in which he had been engaged for many years. In an earlier manuscript version, it served as the data base of *loci classici* from which he drew his citations for the *De Pictura Veterum*. In August, 1677 Junius moved for the last time, into the house of his nephew Isaak Vossius, Gerhard's son, who had come over to Windsor four years before as residentiary canon. There he died, tended by his nephew and his sister Elizabeth, on November 19, 1677, at the Methusalan age of 88 years.

That we know so little of Junius's long life apart from his whereabouts and the list of his books only indicates how much he was absorbed in his scholarly work and how little involved in anything outside the library. With few exceptions, his letters, when they do not deal with the small duties of family obligation, are concerned with his reading, his writing, and the fate of his publications. In a life of the author prefixed to the edition of 1694, Graevius tells us that, with no wife or child to make claims on his time, Junius devoted himself to his scholarship with monastic regularity. He would rise daily at four, study until breakfast, and then, before returning to his books, either take a long walk or a run across the fields for the sake of his health (a Van Dyck portrait of Junius at forty-nine clearly indicates the trim figure and pinched cheeks of a veteran runner). According to Graevius, in bad weather this pioneer of aerobic fitness would climb up and down the stairs of his house.

A like intellectual stamina is reflected in the sheer volume of Junius's life work. As we have noted, The *De Pictura Veterum* appeared in 1637, an English version following the next year, and, after that, a further translation by the author into Dutch. This compendium of the literary sources of the visual arts in antiquity, meticulous and exhaustive as it is, nonetheless represents a detour from the main line of Junius's philological scholarship in Gothic, Anglo-Saxon and Old Germanic texts.

Among his publications in this field, including versions of the Gospels in Gothic and Anglo-Saxon, the most influential proved to be the *Caedmonis monachi paraphrasis poetica geneseos* (1655), Junius's edition of an Anglo-Saxon version of Genesis based on a manuscript given to him by Archbishop Ussher. Although Junius's belief that this "poetic paraphrase" was written by the monk Caedmon is no longer credited, the manuscript (now Bodleian MS. Junius II) entered the modern canon of Old English literature in the edition of 1931 by G.P.Krapp. Still known as the Junius manuscript, it contains three other poems besides the Genesis: *Daniel*, *Christ and Satan*, and an epic version of Exodus.

As medieval scholars well know, the Genesis poem—2936 lines in the Junius manuscript—combines two distinct works referred to as Genesis A and B. B is a fragment of about six hundred lines dating from the ninth century and interpolated into the longer A text, thought to have been written two hundred years earlier. Junius's association with Genesis B has also brought him to the attention of Miltonists, who have noted a number of parallels between the Old English retelling of the Fall and *Paradise Lost*. With some evidence at hand that Milton and Junius had at least made each other's acquaintance (*Milton Encyclopedia*, p. 175), it is intriguing to think that the poet whose fascination with origins included an interest in early Britain—and who in the 1640s had considered writing an "Arthuriad" before turning to the story of the Fall—would have found the conjunction of the Biblical and the British represented by Genesis B compelling. Would Milton, whose knowledge of Old English was halting at best, have missed the opportunity of discussing this manuscript with the foremost expert in England?

Junius's other interest in what would become, largely through his example, the discipline of classical art history, is less well known to literary critics than his contributions to Anglo-Saxon philology. Yet the remarkable fact about a work so little read today as the *De Pictura Veterum* is that until the time of Lessing it stood as the authoritative account of the visual arts in antiquity, its influence pervasive well into the eighteenth century, and not only in England but throughout Europe. Here in a single volume was everything the ancients had said on the subject of painting and sculpture, both a record of specific works and a compendium of anecdotes and theoretical statements gleaned from a wide range of sources. Rubens set the tone in his letter of congratulations to Junius, praising the book on its Latin publication in 1637 as "a generously proffered hoard of all the examples, the opinions, and the tenets promoting the dignity and splendor of the Art of Painting which the ancients enshrined in their literature" (Aldrich, I, 327).Edward Norgate, who traveled on the continent as an Arundel buyer and tutored Arundel's sons in painting, depends heavily on Junius in his *Miniatura*, written between 1648 and 1650.

In subsequent English discussions of the origins and purposes of art, the use of Junius's book often verges on plagiarism. William Sanderson's *Graphice* (1658) takes nearly all its theoretical passages from the *De Pictura*, while, in the age of Pope, both Henry Bell's *Historical Essay on the Origins of Painting* (1728) and George Turnbull's *Treatise on Ancient Painting* (1740) are also based largely on Junius. On the continent the treatise was later available in Junius's 1641 Dutch translation as well as in the posthumous Latin edition of 1694 brought out by Graevius. The influence of Junius has been traced to the allegory of the artistic rivalry depicted in Velázquez's *Las Hilanderas* (Bedaux), to the "motions of the countenance" in Rembrandt's early portraiture (Schwartz), and to the conceit of the speaking likeness in seventeenth-century Dutch portraiture generally (Ford). It extends as far as the conception of the artist's purpose in J.M.W. Turner, who in 1809 took notes, still preserved, on his reading of Junius (Ziff). In Italy the book continued to be cited as late as 1821as the best work of its kind (see Aldrich, I, lxvii n.108).

One reason for the remarkable durability, as well as the wide influence, of Junius's work is that it could be made to serve opposite purposes in the ongoing debate between the "ancients" and the "moderns." On the side of the ancients, the book offered an exhaustive record of Greek and Roman commentary on the visual arts, and it argued not only for the genius of classical painting but for its achievement of a comprehensive and divinely inspired theory of art. In this account, the "ancients" lose their historical specificity and speak as one, with a corporate and timeless voice, authorizing all future practice by their precept and example. The movement of history only removes us farther from the source of this original perfection. Thus, in France, Junius's book spurred the cult of the antique associated with Fréart de Chambrais in the mid-seventeenth century and helped to shape the aesthetic program of the French Academy (Salerno 242).

Despite his prestige as an antiquarian, however, "Junius is at one with Bacon's and Vasari's conceptions of history in adopting the theory of progress, and he, too, discerns in the antique the infancy of art, every art being imperfect in its beginnings. Thus, only one colour was used at first, then four, and in modern times all were used in their infinite variety" (Salerno 239). So, Junius argues, "the most renowned Artificers, should never have obtained the glory of that name, if taking courage they had not hoped still to doe better then the best of their predecessors" (15). As scholars have observed, Junius unproblematically joins the "chronological" and the "systematic," the historical and the ahistorical (Ellenius 50; see also Warnke, 136–139). With little interest in establishing clear chronologies or lines of influence, or even of distinguishing between Greek and Roman art within what is for him the homogeneous space of "antiquity," he can hardly be said to be writing a history of art at all, at least as such an enterprise would come to be understood only after Winckelmann. Neither an "historian" or an "antiquary" as those terms were understood in the seventeenth century (see Woolf), he rather applied the skills of the philologist to the task set for him by Arundel. Junius will have it both ways: the arts move boldly forward toward their ultimate perfection, later painters and sculptors improving in turn upon the cruder productions of those who came before; but that perfection is itself theorized and substantially achieved in antiquity. Thus Junius could be cited as a champion of antiquity and progress alike, and his prestige in either cause was enhanced by the evident thoroughness of his researches. Whatever the contradictions of such a scheme, and whatever the weakness of his compilation as an historical record from our own point of view, his accomplishment on the face of it was a triumph of Baconian industriousness in the collection of evidence. The *De Pictura Veterum*, accompanied after 1694 by the *Catalogus*, offered a plenary and comprehensive work, in D.C. Allen's phrase a "great alphabet of art," that could satisfy the most encyclopedic appetite for knowledge about classical painting and sculpture (265).

From the point of view of the history of artistic theory, Junius's key role in compiling such an impressive archive of classical passages was the claim to have documented the ancient affiliation of the verbal and pictorial arts more thoroughly than ever before: "'All Arts,' sayth *Tullie*, 'that doe belong to humanitie, have a common band, and are ally'd one to another, as by a kind of parentage'" (45: I cite the Junius's English translation of 1638, unless otherwise noted). To be sure, Junius's argument for the "sisterhood" of the arts, coming late in the day of Renaissance commentary on the interrelation of poetry and painting, is hardly original. The oft-repeated Horatian tag *ut pictura poesis*, which was thought to proclaim the rule, "as in painting, so in poetry," was a venerable Renaissance commonplace. So, too, was the sentence of Simonides declaring that painting was a "silent poesy" and poetry a "speaking picture." Generations of Renaissance schoolboys had honed their skills in argument by taking one side and then the other in the venerable *paragone* between the arts: Which is "better," poetry or painting? The debate presupposes that the two arts are contesting a common ground. As early as the 1430s Alberti had advised painters to associate with poets if they wanted to put their art on a sound theoretical basis, and thanks to a number of modern scholars working in the line of Hagstrum, Lee, and Baxandall, we have a detailed critical history of the Renaissance appropriation of Greek and Roman literary and rhetorical commentary for the purposes of a nascent art history. In the absence of a body of classical art theory as such, whatever the ancients had to say about poetry could, it was assumed, be profitably applied to the plastic arts.

Junius's influence lay not in his originality on this point, but rather in the copiousness of his sources. To "prove" the "mutual relation there is between *Poesie* and *Picture*" (45), Junius provides a cascade of citations to Cicero, Tertullian, Ovid, Pliny, the "Peripatetike Philosophers," Horace and Quintilian, all in the space of two pages (44–46), to be followed in the course of his discussion by Hermogenes, Philostratus, Dio Chrysostom, Diogenes Laertes, Saint Basil, Seneca, Saint Gregory, Valerius Maximus, and a procession of others adduced to lend their support. The effect of this tireless quotation as a feature of Junius's writing will be considered below in another context, but here it is enough to note the massive sense of authority created by the sheer preponderance of such evidence, however arguably pertinent it may be piece by piece to the doctrine Junius works so hard to support.

His one further step, again building on Cicero and Quintilian, was to shape this material into an art of painting based upon the *partes orationis* of ancient rhetoric. The affiliation between rhetoric and painting would similarly demonstrate the "sisterhood" of the arts. When the ancients brought painting "to the height of a perfect and accomplished Art," they "observed in Picture these five principall points":

> Invention, or Historicall argument. Proportion, or Symmetrie. Colour, and therein Light and Shadow, as also Brightnesse and Darknesse. Motion or Life, and therein Action and Passion. Disposition, or an Oeconomicall placing and ordering of the whole worke. (221–222)

As Colette Nativel has argued, this division is roughly parallel to that proposed for rhetoric by Cicero in the *De Oratore*, with "Invention" and "Disposition" common to both arts, "Proportion" and "Colour" equivalent to the orator's *elocutio*, and "Motion" to action (20). It also may be seen to correspond to the five-part division of architecture found in Vitruvius (Salerno 242). To conflate the arts in this formal way is to emphasize both the prestige of painting and its systematic coherence in relation to oratory and architecture as well as poetry, all stemming in a clear genealogical line from the same "parentage." It also enables Junius to establish the importance of painting as a vivid force for instruction in virtue, as David Howarth observes (*Images of Rule* 284). No mere indulgence, the lavish expenditures of a collector like Arundel must therefore be appreciated as a cultural enterprise of the highest moral and intellectual purpose.

However, as this particular strand of the narrative of art history is drawn out from Junius, through Winckelmann, and to Lessing, the plot requires that Junius be overthrown as the chief proponent of a theory that, as it was seen from a later vantage point, could only lead to a confusion of the arts. As is well known, in the *Laocoön* (1766) the German dramatist and critic Gotthold Ephraim Lessing takes it as his task to disentangle poetry and painting on formal grounds, arguing that "succession of time is the province of the poet just as space is that of the painter" (91). Lessing is also at pains to correct the mistaken historical assumption of a sisterhood of the arts in antiquity. Thus, although he much admires the "boundless reading" and "perceptive knowledge of art" in Winckelmann's *Geschichte der Kunst des Alterthums* published two years before his own book, Lessing finds that on the question of the interrelation of poetry and painting, even his great countryman fell into error by blindly following Junius in misrepresenting the evidence of the classical canon:

> In his writing on the imitation of Greek works of art Herr Winckelmann had previously let himself be misled several times by Junius. Junius is a very decep-

> tive author; his entire work is a *cento*, and because he always attempts to use the language of the ancients, he not infrequently applies to painting passages from them which refer in their original context to anything but painting. (153)

Where, for example, Longinus had said that the end of the imagination in poetry was to astonish, but that of *oratory* was to make vivid, "Junius substitutes painting for rhetoric; and it was in his writings and not in Longinus' that Herr Winckelmann read: '*Praesertim cum Poeticae phantasiae finis sit* [...], *Pictoriae vero*" (154, citing *De pictura veterum* I.4). Lamentably, "various inaccuracies in the *History of Art* have arisen simply because in his haste Herr Winckelmann consulted Junius rather than the primary sources" (155).

It is noteworthy that Junius's reputation in the developing field of classical art history is still formidable more than a century after his book appeared, but he survives as the defender of an earlier aesthetic that had (mis)read the ancient authors under a strong presumption of the consanguinity of poetry and painting, and he must now stand convicted of perpetuating a deception. In the century between Junius and Lessing, it has been argued, the evolving disciplines of art- and literary history had become more proprietary and more concerned with protecting boundaries. Lessing's argument represents a formal acknowledgment of that territoriality (on the "politics of genre" in Lessing, see Mitchell, Ch. 4). Selden, we recall, had imagined the parts of learning as islands and continents, each offering a prospect onto the rest, none so far from its neighbors "but that, from some shore of it, another may be discovered" and "possessed." For Lessing, any attempt to combine two moments separate in time into a single painting is "an intrusion of the painter into the domain of the poet," while any attempt to create a visual effect in poetry by enumerating the parts of a scene better grasped "at one glance," is "an intrusion of the poet into the domain of the painter" (91). With the arts now separated into formal "domains," Junius ceases to be a reliable guide to the field. Insofar as his own work facilitates the collection of antiquities by men like Arundel, Junius is partly responsible for his own demise The very competition for artworks associated with particular geographical domains (Greece, the Levant) reflects and abets the larger project of European expansion into new territories whose markets must be protected against foreign intrusion. After Graevius in 1694, and aside from a 1972 facsimile of the 1638 English version of *The Painting of the Ancients*, there was no new edition of Junius until that published by Keith Aldrich and Philipp and Raina Fehl in 1991.

In returning to a text so little read today, we reclaim a crucial work produced the Arundel circle, as well as one of extraordinary importance in laying the groundwork for the fields of classical art history. Paradoxically, we also confront a text often so dense with quotation and citation as, for long stretches, to be virtually unreadable. *The Painting of the Ancients* is divided into three books, setting forth, according to the plan outlined by Junius on the title page, the "Beginning, Progresse, and Consvmmation of that most Noble Art." The third book contains the scheme analyzed by Nativel, the "five principall points" observed by the ancients at the height of their art—Invention, Proportion, Color, Motion or Life, and Disposition—as well as a discussion of "a certain kind of Grace" which brings all five into a "mutual accord" (221–22). Within this orderly frame, however, Junius's text presents itself exactly as Lessing had described it, or dismissed, it: a *cento* or pastiche of quotations.

Thus, in a typical passage, Junius is pursuing a point found in Pliny, that "Grecian children by an usuall custome of the Country did first of all beginne with the rudiments of these Arts [carving and painting]." He continues :

> [I]t shall not seeme strange to any one that weigheth the fore-mentioned words of *Plinie*, why *Sicyon* is called by the same Author *patria picturae*, that is, *the native Country of picture.* So sayth *Strabo* likewise, that *the Arts of Painting and Carving, with all such kinde of workmanship, were most of all augmented at* Corinth *and* Sicyon. Of *Corinth* sayth *Orosius*, that *for the space of many generations it hath been a shop of all* Arts *and* Artists, *yea a common* Marttowne *of* Asia *and* Europe. Of *Sicyon,* see *Plutarch* in the life of *Aratus. Sidonius Apollinaris* sayth that *Greece was famous for* Painters *and* Carvers. And *Plinie* termeth the Grecians *pingendi fingendiq[ue] conditores,* that is, *founders of painting and casting.* (99)

The matter at hand—that the fame of Sicyon proves the importance of early training in the arts—is nearly buried under the weight of authoritative testimony, belaboring a point no one would dispute. As the narrative here collapses back into a list of citations (with all references meticulously noted in the margins), Junius's text betrays its origins in the catalogue of classical passages on art that would be published after the author's death. Like the Corinth of old cited in this passage, *The Painting of the Ancients* is a "common Mart-towne" of all arts and artists where Pliny, Strabo, Orosius, Plutarch, Sidonius Apollinaris and (as the account continues) a hundred others gather and jostle for space. But the effect of Junius's own "workmanship" in assembling this *omnium gatherum* is not a babble of voices or a pouring forth of the contents of the archive—as it is, for example, in Robert Burton, who famously compares his style to a river (1.32).

Rather, Junius seems to be engaged in piling on, his own researches continuing the same process of augmentation as the arts enjoyed at Corinth and Sicyon. The style is a building project, a strenuous exercise in *aedificatio.* Here, in a passage appropriately about the rudiments of Greek education, Junius excavates and reassembles the scattered fragments of antiquity into a unified structure by fitting the sayings of the various authors into a piece of stonework Jonsonian in its solidity. What may "seeme strange" to the reader will become familiar when he "weigheth...the words" laid into the fabric of the page. Junius appeals to a judicious reader, one capable of weighing the evidence rationally, but also to a reader who will feel in this text the sheer preponderance of the words brought to bear. "What weight, and what authoritie in thy speech" (31): Jonson's praise in the famous epigram on his own schoolmaster, William Camden, the author of *Britannia,* may apply to Junius. Both produce works of massive erudition, and both speak with the full weight of the *auctoritates* they have labored to compile.

In this respect, the authority claimed by Junius's book is both more confident and less complex and self conscious than Burton's in the *Anatomy of Melancholy*, the other great learned compilation of the age, originally published in 1621 and, coincidentally, reissued by Burton in a fourth edition in 1638, the year of Junius's English translation of the *De Pictura.* The comparison is instructive. Burton describes his own book, as Lessing would Junius's, as a *cento*, and in doing so he employs a simile that recalls the literal meaning of the term as a "patchwork":

> As already, we shall have a vast chaos and confusion of books, we are oppressed with them, our eyes ache with reading, our fingers with turning. For my part I am one of the number, *nos numerus sumus:* I do not deny it, I have only this of Macrobius to say for myself, *Omne meum, nihil meum,* 'tis all mine, and none mine. As a good housewife out of diverse fleeces weaves one piece of cloth, a bee gathers wax and honey out of many flowers, and makes a new bundle of all, *Floriferis ut apes in saltibus omnia libant,* I have laboriously collected this cento out of divers writers, and that *sine iniuria,* I have wronged no authors, but given every man his own[.] (1.24–25)

It is a gesture of self-deprecation: the work is merely a quilt, a homely product of the housewife's craft, of which Burton provides an example by weaving "divers writers," including a strand of Lucretius on the bees, into the very definition of this "cento." The author is merely a collector, a hard-working Baconian bee gathering the sweets of others—"and that *sine iniuria*," while doing them no harm. Yet as every reader knows from the sheer heft of the volume, this modest effort is gargantuan in its ambition. It makes claims for a self not only large enough to contain contradictions (as Montaigne had said of his own essays), but one capable of ranging, as Ruth Fox notes in her study of the *Anatomy*, from "the pharmacopoeia of a medical treatise to a consolation of philosophy, from satirical denunciations of human folly to sermons on charity and despair, from analyses of man's physiology to descriptions of the cosmos or of the workings of good and evil spirits" (6).

In such a vast undertaking, in which everything is taken from others, but in which every man is given "his own"—that is, quoted in his own words and properly cited—what remains as Burton's "own"? Burton returns again and again, sometimes playfully and sometimes with an edge, to the paradox of ownership: "No news here; that which I have is stolen from others, *Dicitque mihi mea pagina, fur es*" (1.22), "My own page cries out to me, You are a thief." As Burton's annotation reminds us, it is the voice of Martial who here cries out to accuse the author of thievery from his own page (my ambiguity is intentional). But then Martial himself, in whose text this line originally appeared, must stand under the same indictment: who did Martial steal it from? In this hall of mirrors, the history of writing recedes into a history of plagiarism, as it does also in the line from Macrobius worked into the passage quoted above: "I have only this of Macrobius to say for myself, *Omne meum, nihil meum,* 'tis all mine, and none mine." It must be "all mine" if it is none of Macrobius's, but if it is Macrobius who says it is "all mine," how can Burton have anything to say "for myself"? As a Lacanian *avant la lettre* Burton plays with the perception that "Language does not arise from within the individual, it is always out there in the world outside.... Language always 'belongs' to another person." (Lacan 5)

The realization that one is always speaking another's words is both a pitfall and a refuge. If Burton's sometimes frantic hilarity is thought "too light and comical for a divine," he will "presume to answer, with Erasmus in like case, 'Tis not I, but Democritus, *Democritus dixit*: you must consider what it is to speak in one's own or another's person...and what liberty those old satirists have had; it is a cento collected from others; not I, but they that say it" (1.121). Like Erasmus in "like case," that is, like Erasmus assuming the *persona* of "Folly" in the *Encomium Moriae*, Burton shifts in and out of the mask of "Democritus Junior." As an authority he inhabits neither himself nor Democritus, but some unmarked space between the two. Indeed, as Democritus *Junior*, he is in perennial tutelage—the son who can never succeed the father in the line of authority because he is either totally claimed by him ("all mine") or else disowned ("none mine").

Faced with an unassimilable inheritance, "a vast chaos and confusion of books," it is no wonder that we are "oppressed with them." Burton's remedy for this melancholy oppression, however, cannot be Bacon's rejection of authority in the interest of starting the project of knowledge afresh. Far from opposing authority, as Sharon Seelig remarks, "No man ever loved it more: Burton cites authorities enthusiastically for one position, and then, just as enthusiastically, for the opposing position" (110). Characteristically, Burton answers the challenge to his own authority by asserting himself in the voice of Erasmus—another, more prestigious authority—in order to assume, in turn, the voice of Democritus, of whom someone, "not I," says, "Democritus said it." If one allows the mind to spiral down into the depths of this vertiginous sentence, one may feel, with Burton, the burden of the past as itself a chief source of melancholy. All those books clogging not only our libraries but our toilets—*non tam refertae bibliothecae quam cloacae*, according to Democritus (1.23)—become, for Burton, the fundamental affliction of scholars. Pity the unfortunate sufferer "of whom Felix Plater speaks, that thought he had some of Aristophanes' frogs in his belly, still crying

Brecececex, coax, coax, oop, oop, and for that cause studied physic seven years, and traveled over most part of Europe to ease himself" (1.21). Such is the chronic indigestion of the writer of centos.

Avoiding facetiousness and despair, Junius manages to steer a much calmer course through his own sources than the bipolar Burton, but the same questions about authority so pointedly foregrounded by Burton's self-conscious ironies also shadow Junius's *Painting of the Ancients*, as they do Arundel's relation to antiquity. By what right can the collector claim the artifacts he acquires as his own? The question runs parallel to that facing Junius as the wholesale importer of the ancients' language. Junius's practice as the compiler of a scholarly cento harks back to the sources of this peculiar and various form as a means, not only of solidifying one's own position by direct reference to the past, but also of appropriating the past—that which one cannot "own"—to a new context. Burton recognizes this effect as well, arguing that "The matter is theirs most part, and yet mine, *apparet unde sumptum sit* [it is plain whence it was taken] (which Seneca approves), *aliud tamen quam unde sumptum sit apparet* [it appears nonetheless as something different than it was in the place from which it was taken]" (1.25).Lessing would charge that Junius's habit of quoting out of context amounts to willful misinterpretation, but any patch sewn into a new fabric will look different however carefully it was cut from its former place. To a greater or lesser extent, the cento carries the covert force of a typological rereading of past texts—subsuming them to a future intention—even as it makes the overt claim to remain faithful to their origina: *apparet unde sumptum sit.* Burton's double gesture here solicits Seneca's approval by quoting the Roman's words as independent and authoritative support for his own position, while at the same time it claiming Seneca's words as "mine" to use as I wish.

The history of the cento supplies a context in which Junius's appropriation of his sources can be appreciated more fully. This sometimes bizarre genre includes a sprinkling of brief examples from pagan late antiquity in which Virgilian hexameters are snipped apart and reassembled, often for the sake of parody, as in the erotic *Cento nuptualis* of Ausonius (c. 374)—one of those Loeb texts in which the editor has chosen to leave the most lubricious passages untranslated. The bedroom scene, Ausonius confesses, or boasts, will make even Virgil immodest. In a prefratory letter, Ausonius belittles his own poem as a "trifling and worthless little book," but in the same gesture he notes at least the merit of its connection to the *ars memorativa:* "'Tis a task for the memory only, which has to gather up scattered tags and fit these mangled scraps together [*solae memoriae negotium sparsa colligere et integrare lacerata*]" (371). The *Cento nuptualis* is, in its way, a commemoration of Virgil, one calling forth the reader's powers of memory as well as the poet's, for the device will only work for an audience that knows its Vergil well enough by heart to recognize all the bits and pieces. Ausonius goes on to describe the process of composition as a kind of game, like that known as the *loculus Archemedius*, in which triangular puzzle pieces of different sizes can be fit together in various ways so as to make pictures of countless objects: "a monstrous elephant, a brutal boar, a goose in flight, and a gladiator in armour," and many more (375; cf Appendix, 394–96).

But it is a game that for all its haphazard appearance requires great technical skill in the joining of verses so as to preserve the meter and the sense, or rather to create them from the random pieces at hand. "It is a poem compactly built [*structura solidatur*] out of a variety of passages and different meanings, in such a way that either two half-lines are jointed together to form one, or one line and following half with another half. For to place two (whole) lines side by side is weak" (372). This is verbal brickwork, where the running courses must overlap to give the structure its solidity. Done well, it results in what Shakespeare's Hippolyta might have called something of great constancy: "And so this little work, the *Cento*, is handled in the same way as the game described," continues Ausonius, "so as to harmonize different meanings, to make pieces arbitrarily connected seem naturally related, to let foreign elements show no chink of light between [*aliena ne interluceant*], to prevent the far-fetched from proclaiming the force which united them, the closely packed from bulging unduly, the loosely knit from gaping" (37). A new work lay torn and dispersed in an old one—in this instance, a bawdy epithalamion in the august *corpus* of Virgil—ready to be made whole again in the cento.

In a more serious vein, this work of recollection and reintegration, Ausonius's *memoriae negotium sparsa colligere et integrare lacerata,* provided the impetus for Christian writers to experiment with the cento as a means of harmonizing pagan learning with Christian doctrine. The *Christus patiens*, a tragedy made of up 2,602 Greek iambic verses lifted from seven plays of Euripedes, was attributed to Saint Gregory of Nazianzus (329?–389); Junius's uncle Vossius was one of a number of Renaissance scholars to debate the question of authorship of this work, long regarded as a key example of Christian tragedy (Tuiliert 19, 13). In Ausonius's lifetime the poetess Falconia Proba stitched 694 Virgilian verses into a *Cento Virgilianis* paraphrasing parts of the Old and New Testaments. In the fifth century the Empress Eudocia, wife of Theodosius II, completed an even more enterprising Homeric cento of nearly 2,500 lines taken from the *Iliad* and the *Odyssey* and recounting the history of the world from the creation to the resurrection of Christ. In this work the infant Jesus is described in a line from the *Odyssey* (9.190) about the Cyclops: "For he was a marvelous thing to behold" (Usher 65). The Wedding at Cana is celebrated in lines taken from various scenes of Homeric feasting and sacrifice (Usher 107). When Mary laments over her dead Son, within a twenty-four-line passage of the poem (ll. 2040–264) "she embraces and addresses him as Briseis does Patroclus (2141–2; 2064), weeps for him as Thetis for Achilles (2044, 2048), faints, recovers, and pronounces a moving elegy like Andromache at Hector's funeral (2046; 2058–61; 2065–7) and mourns her son's trip to Hades as Anticleia does Odysseus's (2049–51; 2062–3)" (Usher 140). To take note, finally, of an example contemporary with Junius, in 1634, three years before *De Pictura*, the indefatigable Alexander Ross published a cento of fifteen hundred lines on the life of Christ entitled *Virgilius Evangelisans, Sive historia Domini et Salvatoris Jesu Christi, Virgilianis verbis et versibus descripta.*

These influential centos clearly indicate how an Ausonian trifle could become the instrument of a powerful typological poetics far subtler in its implications than the cut-and-paste procedure of the form might suggest. Christians might find the Word of God adumbrated not just in the Fourth Eclogue, the *locus classicus* of supposed Christian prophecy, but, potentially, in any and every word written by the "Evangelist" Virgil. Just as the Virgin has her Old Testament predecessors in Eve,

Sara, Rachel, and Rebecca, she also has her pagan antitypes in Briseis, Thetis, Andromache, and Anticleia. The patchwork cento literalizes the idea that these forerunner texts, classical as well as Hebrew, are folded into the Gospel. The Virgin's grief, in Eudocia's poem, expresses itself through and fulfills the historical grief of a chorus of Homeric women, whose laments for the dead would prove to be far more profound in the fullness of Christian time than they, or their pagan creator, could have possibly known. Thetis's lament for Achilles is "all hers," in that it is rooted in the Homeric world and preserved intact in the Christian narrative, but it is finally "none hers" when it is assumed by the Virgin and perfected in her—Mary's—lament for Christ.

Thus the cento not only sutures the words of the classics into a Christian narrative, it sutures two historical eras, the period of pagan antiquity and the period of the Church. From an unsympathic point of view, it may seem that a poet like Eudocia only does violence to the classical text. In an essay on "The Greek Christian Poets" published in 1842, Elizabeth Barrett Browning imagines the Empress sitting "among the ruins of the holy city, addressing herself most unholily with whatever good intentions and delicate fingers, to pulling Homer's gold to pieces bit by bit" (qtd. Usher 1; see also Taplin 100–102). Eudocia's implicit comparison of the Cyclops to the baby Jesus (both of them "marvelous...to behold") seems to embarrass even her modern commentator, who notes that the line in question from the *Odyssey* is "used here with considerable *Verfremdung*" (Usher 65). But this estrangement from the source, however extreme in this instance, is in fact the condition of the cento. For Ausonius, as we have seen, all the lines collected for the cento are *aliena*, "foreign elements" in their new setting—literally "far fetched." Hence the measure of the artist's skill lies in fitting them so snugly together that the "force which united them" is not apparent, thus recuperating and naturalizing what had become, to the Christian centoist, historically and theologically alien.

Surely the most memorable expression of the centoist's ambition in Junius's lifetime is Milton's call in the *Areopagitica* for the faithful to "unite those dissevered pieces which are yet wanting to the body of Truth":

> Truth indeed came once into the world with her divine Master, and was a perfect shape most glorious to look on. But when he ascended, and his apostles were laid asleep, then straight arose a wicked race of deceivers, who, as that story goes of the Egyptian Typhon with his conspirators, how they dealt with the good Osiris, took the virgin Truth, hewed her lovely form into a thousand pieces, and scattered them to the four winds. From that time ever since the sad friends of Truth, such as durst appear, imitating the careful search that Isis made for the mangled body of Osiris, went up and down gathering up limb by limb still as they could find them. (741–42)

Itself an implicit or indirect cento, the passage inserts the "story…of the Egyptian Typhon" into the main thread of the argument about the fate of Truth after the time of Christ. In doing so, it also makes an historical connection between the Christian mystery of the incarnation and the pagan mystery of the *sparagmos* of Osiris, whose "mangled body" dimly foretold both the sufferings of the cross and the subsequent laceration and dispersion of the body of truth.

Writing in very much the same vein, in the Latin dedication to King Charles in the 1637 edition of his book, Junius also imagines himself in the role of Isis:

> A keen desire took hold of me to collect the lessons of the Ancients, which are now, as it were, severed from the body of the theory of art and bit by bit dispersed among the literary remains of Classical Antiquity, and to arrange the pieces in such a way as to arrive at the contours of true art; my hope being that once I had, to some degree at least, grasped in my mind the likeness of the art of the Ancients, or at least a shadow of its likeness, I might the better become equipped to comprehend the beauty of these most commendable arts themselves. (Aldrich I, 319)

This desire heralds a "bit by bit" recovery of the past, but also a theoretical ascent towards the mind's comprehension of beauty itself, as reflected in the "shadow of its likeness" cast across the historical record. As Pico had earlier put it, comparing the ascent and descent of the philosophical mind to the "angels going up and down on Jacob's ladder," we "shall sometimes ascend, with the force of Phoebus collecting the parts like the limbs of Osiris into a unity, until, resting at last in the bosom of the Father who is above the ladder, we shall be made perfect with the felicity of theology" (230). To the Christian centoist, the myth of Osiris itself recollects an originary and singular perfection that preceded pagan culture: a Truth dispersed and obscured in alien exile, awaiting the redemptive labors of Isis. Junius's faith in the possibility of recovering a pristine "body of the theory of art" by arranging the pieces of classical antiquity prompts him to undertake the same labors in the realm of the aesthetic.

In the light of the poems we have been glancing at, Junius's *Painting of the Ancients*, as well as the passage above from Milton, can be regarded as *centi* in prose. Junius's habit of stitching his style with quotations combines the technique of the verse cento with the more general tendency of Renaissance scholarly prose to authorize itself by the copious citation of the authorities, and so to produce the macaronic effect also found in Burton, Donne, Jonson, Milton and many others of juxtaposing English and Latin passages, or of conjoining a distinctively English vernacular with a Latinate diction. The "inkhorn" controversies of the Elizabethan period record an earlier debate as to whether vernacular prose should establish itself as a cento-like combination of Latinate and homespun terms, or strive for something more purely "English." It was only in the eighteenth century, when the question of cultural authority had been largely resolved in favor of the "moderns," that English prose also took on its modern form, uncumbered of its onetime collection of verbal antiquities. The "modern" writer is free from the double bind of a heaviliy citational style. The centoist's rewoven material is always "theirs most part, and yet mine": a dilemma which, in *The Painting of the Ancients*, helps us to understand the kind of cultural work accomplished by the massive incorporation of classical commentary into Junius's text.

The history of the verse cento forces us to ask what we mean, what we *can* mean, when we speak the words of another—a crucial question in early modern constructions of the past long before its most recent appearance as a postmodern concern. It heightens the anxieties (of authority, originality, and appropriation) surrounding the practice of *imitatio*, of which the cento reflects at once the purest instance but perhaps the most tainted motive: *Dicitque mihi mea pagina, fur es*, "my own page says to me, you are a thief." The cento thus reminds us that the apparently mechanical and unsignficant act of quotation sets up complex resonances between the source text and its destination in the page that "speaks"—including, for example, Browning's implication that the Empress's pulling Homer apart "bit by bit" enacts the Christian's revenge on the classical golden age. At the same time, for Christians looking back, there must have been an aching Benjaminian pathos in their survey of the remains of classical antiquity. Like the Empress Eudocia "among the ruins," Junius is faced with the task of reconstructing just such a fragmented past. His collecting of quotations arises from the same syncretic desire that led Renaissance philosophy to piece together all the ancient schools into a single truth within the frame of the Gospels; from this point of view, Ficino's *Platonic Theology* is a philosophical cento. Of the great works of classical visual art, little remained except broken architecture, pieces of pottery, defaced coins and dismembered statuary "scattered to the four winds" and unearthed by accident in farmers' fields. What if this mangled body, or at least some simulacrum of it, could be recollected limb by limb from the bits of text that contain the record of it, like an intricate jigsaw puzzle—or its historical antecedent, the Greek *loculus Archemedius*—waiting to be put together again?

In a congratulatory letter published with the Dutch translation of the *De Pictura*, Grotius compared Junius's book to an intricate mosaic made out of many colored *tesserae* but producing, overall, the effect of nature—Junius's "likeness of the art of the Ancients." As Junius's modern editors remark, the figure of the mosaic aptly describes the author's working method of "cutting, pasting, and rewriting" evident in the surviving manuscript of his *Etymologicum Linguae Anglicanum*, now in the Bodleian: "As Junius revised his entries he crossed out sections and pasted flaps with new texts over the parts he wished to replace or expand. Frequently parts from older manuscripts or of pages in print are pasted in or added to a page as a fold-out" (Aldrich 1.lii, n. 69). For the philologist and compiler, the very act of writing literally involves patching materials in a scholarly *Handwerk* that allies his own craft with that of the plastic artists whose history he is attempting to piece together.

From both an historical and a technical point of view, then, one can appreciate Junius's admiration for a story out of the "sacred Records" of the Egyptian priests, related in turn in a passage from Diodorus Siculus. It seems that the famous brother team of sculptors, Telecles and Theodorus, were commissioned to make an "image of *Apollo Pythius* for the inhabitants of *Samos.*" The records report that "*Telecles* made one halfe of that statue in *Samos*, whilest *Theodorus* his brother made the other halfe at *Ephesus*, & that those halfes being brought together did agree so well as if the whole statue had been the workmanship of one and the same hand" (269). This binding agreement, in Junius's book, includes not only the perfect fit between the two halves of a statue carved in different cities. It reflects the consensus of the ancients about the nature and purpose of art (they speak with one voice), Junius's agreement with them, and the "agreement" of all the artifacts of antiquity in supporting this consensus—as well as the proportional fitness obtaining between the painting of the ancients and *The Painting of the Ancients*. The unspoken but fundamental argument of the book is that even in a sprawling, piecemeal archive, a coherent history can be read as the work of "one and the same hand," the handwriting of "the ancients." Searching through the "literary remains" of antiquity, the scholar will continue the patient work of Isis in piecing together the "body" of art there entombed.

Like a wall concealing what lies behind it, however, the very solidity and consonance of Junius's style—its creation of a perdurable monument called *The Painting of the Ancients*—conceals the absence of the actual *painting* of the *ancients*, except for the traces of those artifacts in the literary record. Junius the librarian immerses himself in books and manuscripts and shows very little awareness of, or interest in, contemporary art, even though he works for the greatest connoisseur of the age. In the dedication to Charles he praises the royal collections but candidly admits that the reason he turned his "mind's eye" to his books, apart from Arundel's urging him to take on the task, was that he was no judge of pictures: "Since I had not the ability to relish these delights with my eyes—for they must be educated and well trained for the purpose—I resolved that I must look at what matters with my mind's eye" (Aldrich I.319). He has little if anything to say about the antiquities Arundel had amassed; the task of actually describing the statuary in the Earl's possession was, as we have seen, left to Selden in the *Marmora Arundellia*. In any event, as Francis Haskell observes, even the most careful study by Renaissance historians of the physical remains of antiquity—coins, mosaics, sculpture—"did not seriously alter the fact that, as far as the study of the past was concerned, the triumph of humanism implied the triumph of the word. The image was relegated to a wholly subordinate position as a potential source of evidence" (13–14).

Besides, all the fabled paintings and statues of the ancients are, for Junius, just that: invisible to the eye, and present only to the mind's eye in the literary accounts of Pliny, Diodorus Siculus, Strabo, and a hundred other writers. Of the works described in such sources, what little had not disappeared had been ravaged by time, a process grimly illustrated by the common Renaissance emblems showing Time chomping on a statue, with the motto: *Tempus edax rerum*. The most famous of these objects—the amazing statue of Apollo fashioned by Telecles and Theodorus, or Parhassios's painting of grapes so perfect that it fooled the birds, or Zeuxis's painting of a curtain so perfect that it fooled Parhassios—very likely never existed at all apart from those *loci* in the written record to which the Renaissance turned again and again for its examples of the heights reached by the artists of antiquity.

This would perhaps be too obvious a point to need any emphasis, were it not for Junius's ability to conjure a vivid "likeness" of these works from the recesses of the literary archive. The interest of Renaissance painters in the ekphrastic tradition offers a signal instance of the desire actually to "reproduce" works of art for which only literary descriptions survive. Guided by a detailed passage in Lucian, Botticelli painted the lost "Calumny of Apelles," now in the Uffizi; whether Apelles ever painted a "Calumny of Apelles" cannot be known. Through the mediation of the text of Lucian—a set piece in which the painting of the calumniation of the famous artist is described in detail—the Botticelli is an exact replica of an original that perhaps never was. Leonard Barkan has written of such ekphrases that "the 'reality' of the picture outside the text is almost always suspect in some way." The "Alexandrian authors of the *Eikones* seem to have invented most of the images they were rhetoricalizing; the shield Achilles has a quantity of matter represented on it unlike any shield that existed in Homeric times or could ever exist; and even Alberti, whom we might appeal to as an example of the professional artist writing theory, devotes much of his descriptive power in *De Pictura* to visual objects he has never seen and only knows about from other people's verbal accounts" ("Making Pictures Speak" 134).

Describing the "never seen" is a burden considerably heavier for Junius than for Alberti, who addresses himself to painters and advises them to befriend literary people if they want to learn something about the theoretical foundations of their practice. Rather than referring painting to poetry, Junius is intent on retrieving painting from poetry by somehow representing the whole body of classical visual art through the verbal medium of "Historical Observations and Examples" (Title page). Not content with what Sidney had called the historian's mere "wordish description," his aspiration to configure his text into a kind of image—a mosaic, a jigsaw puzzle—is one he shares with the composers of formal centos. He will replace the "never seen" with a vivid equivalent in words: "In truth, [the aim of] painting is enargeia," an effect which Junius believes the sisterhood of the arts also makes possible for the writer. But the "truth of painting" in Junius's representation of it can only be a *trompe l'oeil.* The trick of the cento, we recall from Ausonius, is to fit the pieces of the puzzle so neatly together, to create so dense and homogeneous and apparently natural a structure, as to leave no chink of light through which the "foreign" elements can be seen: *aliena ne interluceant*. In Junius's case, if you try to pull away the curtain to see what lies behind it—as Parhassios attempted to do with the brilliant *trompe l'oeil* created by his rival Zeuxis—you will discover that there is nothing there. When the cento writer's words attempt to reassemble, or perhaps rather dissemble, a visible body into a "speaking picture," they reveal only that their object is alien indeed, the other that cannot be incorporated into words, and that language can only succeed in bespeaking its absence.

Those with a more passionately iconoclastic streak than Junius might actually revel in the blindness of language, trusting in the power of the Word to shield the faithful from the temptation of the eye. Reformers in the image-breaking tradition of Zwingli and Karlstadt would regard the impermeability of the word to the image not as its defect but as the source of its purity, while the more moderate Luther would advocate whitewashing the walls of churches and decorating them instead with passages from scripture. At the most intense moment in Donne's Good Friday meditation on the Crucifixion, when the Ignatian procedure of the *compositio loci* calls upon the meditator to fix a vivid picture of the scene in his imagination, the poet is "almost…glad" that he does *not* see "That spectacle of too much weight for mee. / Who sees Gods face, that is selfe life, must dye" (336). As I have also argued elsewhere, both the pathos and the triumph of *Samson Agonistes* as Christian tragedy lie, for Milton, not only in the blindness of the hero but in the mysterious darkness of a play never intended for the stage (*Iconoclasm*, ch. 6). In Milton's most telling irony, those illustrious Philistians who perished had the best seats in the house on the occasion of Samson's final performance. When the roof collapsed on them, they were, literally, the victims of a spectacle of too much weight for them, while the messenger who stood "obscure," unnoticed and himself barely able to see the show from a distance, survived to *tell* the tale. The same impulse had led the more radical reformers to deny the "real presence" of Christ's body in the wafer and the wine displayed to the sight of the congregation, affirming instead his "spiritual presence" and arguing that the communion is to be understood symbolically as a verbal memorial of Christ's promise at the Last Supper.

I mention the Eucharistic controversy for three reasons connected to Junius's project and, more generally, to the kind of historical discourse in which both theology and art history are involved. First, the reformist position entails the same sense of visual loss (both of the mass as spectacle, and of the historical event it re-presented immediately and miraculously) and verbal replenishment (by the word as promise and commemoration) as Junius faces in his attempt to remember classical art. Second, that loss, even its polemical form as a repudiation of the loathsome doctrines of popery, engenders mourning and nostalgia, and an awareness that all recoveries are only partial. We have seen that Burton is weighed down by the melancholy realization that the very attempt to reproduce the ancients in their own words on one's own (and not their) page makes one a liar. As Regina Schwartz has argued, even so staunch an opponent of the "cannibalism" of the mass as Milton betrays, in his poetry, a "real hunger" for the body no longer available except in commemorative language, but displaced onto Raphael's keen interest in lunch (*PL* 5.437), during an communion from which the reader is now debarred.

The parallel is apt, too, because Junius seems to have the sacramental question of the "real presence" at the back of his mind at a key moment in *The Painting of the Ancients*, when he urges the modern artist to take his inspiration from the greats of antiquity as well as from "such men as doe deserve his respect" among his own acquaintance:

> Although now reading and study can doe much, yet shal that Artificer bring great spirits to his worke, who beside the most profitable endeavours of an emulating vertue, associateth himselfe with *Apelles, Protogenes, Polycletus, Phidias*; not only considering with himselfe, what these noble soules if they were present, should do or else advise him to doe in the workes he taketh in hand, but propounding also unto himselfe, how they should censure his worke brought to an end .... This conceived presence of antient, and the true presence of moderne masters will do us more good, if wee doe constantly beleeve, that the estimation of these present and following times dependeth on the judgement of those whom we make choice of for the reforming of our works. (250–51)

As in painting, so in Protestantism. The "reforming of our works" seeks its inspiration at the *fons et origo*, in Apelles, Protogenes, Polycletus, and Phidias—the prinstine theologians of the early church of classical art. But their "presence," like that of their lost works, can only be "conceived." To Junius's artificer, the ancients are present at this painterly communion in spirit, as a spiritual presence both more powerful though less palpable than the "true presence" of their successors, the modern masters. But their presence is inevitably mediated by the word, by the words (of others) through which they are recalled. Here Junius cites Longinus: "*Many are carried away by another mans spirit as by a divine inspiration*, sayth he, *even as the report goeth, that* Pythia *the Priest of* Apollo *is suddenly surprised when she approcheth into the trivet: where they say there is an abrupt hole in the ground, breathing forth a divine exhalation; and that the priest filled with their divine power, doth instantly prophecie by inspiration*" (250). For the scholar-priest as well as for the painter, the immediacy of "divine inspiration" at the source, however vividly "conceived," recedes through a series of verbal sources, from Longinus to the "report" on which Longinus relies in his treatise on the sublime, to the even vaguer "they say" by which we are given our only original assurance of the existence of the site of ancient prophecy—the point at which inspiration literally disappears down a "hole in the ground."

Donne says of the original Good Friday "Sacrifice" which he cannot see from the historical (disad)vantage of 1613, "Though these things, as I ride, be from mine eye, / They'are present yet unto my memory." The arts of memory retrieve the past. Even "as I ride" in one direction, memory speeds even more quickly in the other, as it were to return to us that which we had forgotten when we set off on our journey. In this sense, Donne's "yet" means "still," signaling the continuity of historical experience made possible by the persistence of the past in memory. Equally, however, the "yet" may be read as "nonetheless," thus suggesting the latent tension in the lines between "eye" and "memory," as well as the loss entailed in the distance between eye-witness experience and the conceived presence of memory.

If the passage from Junius quoted above were itself an ekphrasis in the style of Lucian or Philostratus, how would we paint the scene of the "The Artist in his Studio" according to the description we have just been given? We would have to show, if not a "great conflux of eager and applauding spectators" crowding in to see the painter's work, at least a more intimate grouping of fellow artists and judicious critics, figures perhaps like Van Dyck, Mytens, Inigo Jones, Peacham, and Junius himself—"such men as doe deserve his respect" (251). Then we would have to find a way of representing those "greater spirits," Apelles and his colleagues from the pantheon of classical art, those "noble souls" from whose inspiration the painter receives advice and censure as "if they were present" (251). Would they appear as historical personages, or allegorical figures, or would their presence be suggested by other means, such as by their fabled masterpieces "recreated" in the artist's studio, as a "painting" by Rubens may be seen to hang on the background wall of a painting by Velázquez? As we have seen, the inclusion of a bust of Homer in Van Dyck's "Madagascar" portrait of Arundel represents one such solution, registering Arundel's antiquarian interest as the counterpart to his interest in a colonial future, as well as the "presence" of a Homeric spirit of epic adventure joining the two. The challenge of conceiving such a painting—of finding a pictorial *concetto* that will put this unseen world before the eye—reflects the ambiguous position of the painter himself, standing between the "conceived presence" of the ancients, and the "true presence" of the modern masters.

This tension between the "conceived presence" and the "true presence" makes itself felt throughout Junius's book as an historical problem inescapable in the attempt to link the ancients and the moderns. Like the two halves of Apollo's statue brought together in a perfect fit, the remote and the immediate must be made to "agree." Again and again, the attempt to capture a "principall beautie" in "conceived things" leads Junius on a paper chase at the end of which the quarry tends to disappear down the rabbit hole: Junius quotes from Proclus's commentary on the *Timaeus* in order to recall the opinion of Plato that the artist who imitates the works of others will never "*attaine to what is perfectly beautifull; seeing the things generated are full of deformed disporportions, and far remoted from the principiall true beautie.*" "*Hence it is,*" Junius/Proclus/Plato continues, "*that* Phidias, *when he made* Jupiter, *did not cast his eye upon any thing generated, but he fetched the patterne of his worke out of a* Jupiter *conceived after* Homers *description*" (19). The true beauty of Phidias's Jupiter here emerges from the remoteness of Junius's sources in a glimpse only long enough for us to see, ironically, that Phidias's conception of it is no less "remoted" than ours, depending as it does on a far distant literary account in Homer.

At the same time, painting has the ability to abolish historical distance, enabling "our mind to enter into a lively consideration of what wee see expressed; not otherwise than if wee were present, and saw not the counterfeited image but the reall performance of the thing" (341). The presence of the past must inform not only "these present" times but also the "following times" if history as such is to be constituted as a field of study (251). The same tension, I want now to argue, runs through Junius's theory of creativity, which commits itself equally to the imitation of nature and to the realization of a conceived ideal as the source of the painter's art.

One strand of Junius's logic leads from the imitation of lower, visible objects to the nobler imitation of an inward truth. "*The arts,*" according to Arnobius, "*are not together with our minds sent forth out of the heavenly places, but all of them are found out here on the earth, and are in processe of time soft and faire forged by a continuall meditation* (29). In the process of the historical development of the arts, painters "doe not onely view but also imitate the wonders of Nature" with increasing proficiency: "*The painters*, sayth *S. Chrysostome, after the mixing of their colours, endeavour to set forth a lively similitude of diverse visible things: thus doe they paint reasonable and unreasonable creatures, trees, warres, battels, streams of blood, pikes, ordinary men....to expresse all manner of visible things*" (4–5). But besides the imitation of natural objects, "we are also to marke another sort of imitation, by which namely the Artificer emboldeneth himselfe to meddle also with such things as doe not offer themselves to the eyes of men" (17–18). These things, "according to *Plato* his opinion," are "prefigured only and represented by the phantasie" (18–19). Pygmalion carved an ivory image of a woman so perfect that, says Ovid, "*it was impossible such a woman should be borne*" (6). Likewise, when Phidias painted his masterpiece of Jupiter and Minerva, according to Cicero "*there did abide in his minde an exquisite forme of beautie, upon the which he staring, directed both his Art and his hand to the similitude of the same*" (20). Inspired by Plato's Ideas, these consummate artists (including the most ancient of the greats such as Phideas and Apelles) are capable of an "absolute" imitation that seems outside the process of historical development altogether: "Such Artificers therefore as carry in their mind an uncorrupt image of perfect beauty, do most commonly powre forth into their workes some certaine glimmering sparkles of the inward beautie contained in their mindes" (6).The same uncorrupt image will also be the source of "that more inward and profound doctrine" that produces the learned painter, instructed, like Apelles, "in all kinde of Sciences, and chiefely in Arithmeticke and Geometry," without which art could not "wel be perfected" (232).

In other passages, however, Junius will martial his authorities to demonstrate that even "conceived" or "intelligible" images must submit to the limits of the visible. The painter's mind, "*as Lucian* speaketh," should be "*like unto a pure, bright looking-glasse,*" receiving the true images of things and not the "monstrous and prodigious Images of things not knowne in nature" such as a conceited wit may devise: "Whatsoever then hath been spoken in the in the former, and also in this present chapter, about the raising of our thoughts and conceits, may not be understood of all sorts of idle and giddie-headed Imaginations, but only of such Phantasies as are grounded upon the true nature of things: *the Art of Painting,* saith *Socrates, is a resembling of visible things* (42). Pursuing this line, Junius arrives at the famous story of Zeuxis, of whom Cicero reports that

> when this noble Artificer intended to leave unto the Inhabitants of Crotona a choice patterne of a most beautifull woman, he did not think it good to seek the perfection of a faultlesse formositie in one particular body; but he pick'd out of the whole City five of the well-favouredst virgins, to the end he might find in

> them that *perfect beauty, which as Lucian* speaketh, *of necessitie must be but one.* (7)

Hardly a model of logical rigor, Junius's theorizing is made up of a cento all the best examples, rather like Zeuxis's composite woman. His most compelling motive is the one here taken from Lucian, that a perfect view of the painter's art, like the perfect beauty which is its object, "of necessitie must be but one," even if the available pieces of it are strewn through all the writers of antiquity.

However unstable the compound, Junius's "one" theory of art combines two fundamental impulses without resolving their apparent inconsistencies. The first, we have seen, insists upon keeping the artist's eye sharply focused on the visible world as he holds the mirror up to nature. This view makes possible a "grounded" history of art as the history of its material and technical development, from its rudimentary beginnings to a perfection based upon the accretion of artistic experience. This empirical emphasis is nonetheless inseparable from an equally strong attraction to the ideal. Thus, the second impulse imagines a conceptual space in which three aspects of the ideal are seen to merge: the Platonic "idea" from which the artist draws his inspiration; our ability to project ourselves *back* into the realm of that idea by forming "a lively consideration of what wee see expressed, not otherwise than if wee were present"; and our corresponding ability to bring the spirit of the artist *forward* as a "conceived presence" in the mind of the contemporary artist or historian. This second impulse thus allows for an ideal history of art, complementing its empirical development and compensating for the sense of loss and dispersion of the visible record of antiquity. At the same time, it preserves the possibility of art's perfection in an essential realm of "inward beautie" not tied to the accidents of history as either progressive or destructive. In this ideal realm, all history is subsumed in a timeless "presence." The distance between the ancient artist and his modern counterpart, as between ancient art and its modern collectors, is abolished. In each other's "presence," the divisive question of what one may claim as one's own dissolves into a transhistorical ideal community. The earliest masters brought painting to perfection by virtue of the "uncorrupt image" of beauty in their minds, and even while raking through the ashes of their achievement scattered in the written record, "certaine glimmering sparkles" of their minds continue to illuminate ours.

3. Junius and Arundel: Collection and Recollection

The "glimmering" of ancient art was, of course, more than a matter of theoretical interest to Arundel, his agents and competitors, as well as to those from whom he made his purchases, whether Levantine dealers or bankrupt Italian counts. We have seen that Arundel himself struck those around him as something of a paradox, a man of sober restraint in his demeanor who nonetheless spent freely on his collections, and whose correspondence preserves the record of two decades of negotiation involving lavish outlays. Obviously sensitive on this point, Junius notes that his patron's matchless collection of drawings is on public view at Arundel house (271), and he would persuade us that, far from being envious of the rich, men of "ordinary estates" should realize how much they benefit from the acquisitions of their betters. They themselves need not "undergoe the charges of buying, since great and generous spirits, furnish their houses with such things not onely for their owne private contemplation, but also for the free use of such as doe professe themselves to be Lovers and well-willers of Art, thinking their cost well bestowed when many doe daily resort to their galleries" (81). Junius also argues with some heat that

> Teastie and ambitiously severe censurers also have but small reason to finde fault with such great and wealthy men as with an excessive cost do buy for strife all manner of Art, valuing the rare works of great Masters according to the delight & contentement they find in the.... Neither is it unlikely that brave and generous men sometimes might resolve of their owne accord to raise the price of Pictures and Statues, because they could not endure that such honest and innoxious delights should be generally condemned and contemned; it seemeth therefore that they have followed the praise-worthy course taken by *Apelles*, when it did grieve him to see how little the rare workes of *Protogenes* were regarded at *Rhodes*. (79–80)

Buying "for strife," or what we might otherwise call a engaging in a bidding war, is justified both as a means of acknowledging the true value of a work of art, and also as a practice with its own historical precedent. For, as we read in Pliny, no less a judge of painting and a connoisseur *avant la lettre* than Apelles insisted on offering fifty talents for the works of Protogenes, far more than the poor price asked by the Rhodian art dealers: "*Neither would Apelles yeeld unto them, till they had raised the price*" (80).

As this passage suggests, Junius is himself following "the praiseworthy course taken by *Apelles*" in working out an economic rationale for collecting just at the moment when, in England, an international art market has sprung up on an unprecedented scale, and when a small group of competitors are buying "for strife" with unprecedented sums at stake. Those of ordinary estates, unschooled in the economics of extraordinary men like Arundel, might well have expected Apelles to haggle with the dealers in Rhodes in order to acquire the "rare" works of Protogenes as cheaply as possible. They do not understand that the value of a work of art is not indexed to market price. Value is intrinsic, and its outward measure is taken only according to the delight it brings to the "Lovers and well-willers of Art." It would be easy to show, Junius argues, that since the arts have always enjoyed the favor of "great Kings and Potentates," artists have not only gotten their "due reward of glory" and—one thinks of Rubens or Van Dyck—an "infinite masse of wealth; yet do we esteeme the mention of such rewards to come far short of the worthines of these Arts, and of the sufficient contentment they doe find in themselves" (15). The importance of wealth to such transactions is frankly acknowledged: "These two things may therfore very wel stand together, That an artificer should chiefely intend the glory of his name, and yet in the second place looke after some reasonable gaine" (190). But any question of gain is to be minimized and sublimated into a system of higher values payable in benevolence, glory, and contentment.

History, according to Junius's reading of his sources, teaches the same lesson, for after "the love of money began to thrust this veneration of Art out of the hearts of men, Artificers also grew thinner and thinner, till none at length were left" (188). When "great and eminent men" who "should have been the supporters of art, grew slack, esteeming their chiefest felicitie to consist in the possession of gold and silver; those arts also which from their greatest good were called Liberall, became servile" (189).Only when the rich spend liberally are the arts redeemed from servitude, and only through such liberal spending is money itself purified or absorbed by the greater value of the "liberal" arts. The deeper distinction here implied between a liberal and a servile culture makes it all the more praiseworthy that benefactors of the arts should allow the "free use" of their collections to others. When the arts are thus supported, furthermore, they offer a rich return on the investment through the accumulation of a kind of imaginative capital, an enterprise in which the artists and the patron or the arts hold a joint interest.

Living in a world of fleeting spectacle—the "burning of a Citie," or the confusion of a shipwreck, both examples coincidentally entailing catastrophic financial loss—art employs the imagination like a diligent provisioner to "lay up carefully what she hath seen, still increasing her store with Images of things unseene" (22). Thus when the collector takes care to furnish his own gallery with a valuable store of paintings, his efforts both emulate and embody the fundamental imaginative investment of art itself. In this vaguely Pauline economics of art, treasures are laid up not on earth but in the imagination, where the deposit will accrue interest if the artist—again supplying a model for the ambitious collector—is bold enough to venture beyond the achievements of his predecessors. "*Nothing*, sayth [Quintilian], *doth receive any encrease by imitation alone,*" but only through the efforts of the artist "*that striveth to goe before*" (30), while Synenius "urgeth that things done by course of custome, must alwayes give place when there are found out things more profitable" (31–32). The competition among collectors buying "for strife" is reflected in, and justified by, the artist's own striving for place. Collecting, even at unaccustomed expense in the short run, is thus rightly seen, not as a sacrifice of the values of art to the marketplace, but as part of an long term "profitable" history connecting the painting of the ancients to the acquisitiveness of the modern connoisseur.

Janus-like, that history looks forward to the advancement of art (when money will have been subsumed into a more perfect appreciation of the value of art), but also backward toward a pristine origin before the world was corrupted by money in the first place. "Looke well into them," says Junius of the great lovers of art, "and you shall take them to be "some remnant of the golden age." There follows an extraordinary reverie, reminiscent of Gonzalo's utopian fantasy in *The Tempest*, on the innocence and purity of spirit of those, like Arundel, who devote themselves to collecting on a magnificent scale:

> They envie no body, they despise no body, they doe not lend their cares to backbiting and slanderous talcs, they doe but imagine well-hung chambers and well-furnished galleries: this doe they make the height of their cares, the height of their wishes, propounding themselves hereafter an innoxious and a happie life. (82)

Like a painting to the artist who conceives it, "well-furnished galleries" are the product of the collector's imagination, not his investment strategy. It is a paradoxical rule of this economic system that spending a great deal of money on art not only vanquishes envy and slander, but renders money itself "innoxious" and virtually invisible, the transparent medium of the imagination. *Beatus ille*: If the vector of secular history leads from the harmony of the golden age to a world of strife, collecting art reverses the process, leading from the strife of acquisition to the enjoyment of an "innoxious and a happie life."

Furthermore, as the example of Apelles as painter/connoisseur also suggests, the art lover and the artificer, both equally possessed of a "well-exercised Imaginative facultie" and the "conceived Images" from which the work of art springs, share an eminent place (also occupied by Junius) as joint custodians of the knowledge of painting. Junius is so insistent on this point that he peremptorily reverses the evident meaning of his source when he comes to consider who is qualified to be a judge of art:

> The younger *Plinie* sayth also expresly, *none but an Artificer can judge of a Painter, Carver, Caster in brasse, or worker in clay.* Observe in the meane time, that in these words of *Plinie* we must understand by the name *Artificer*, not such a workman onely as doth really paint and carve, but such a Lover and well-willer of Art as by a rare and well-exercised Imaginative facultie, is able to conferre his conceived Images with the Pictures and Statues that come neerest unto Nature, and is likewise able to discerne by a cunning and infallible conjecture the severall hands of divers great Masters out of their manner of working. (76)

What we now call art history has not yet emerged as a scholarly discipline justified by its ability to supply a rationale for the field of artistic practice—as, for example, philology had for the field of language—but Junius is preparing the way. What Junius constructs through the composite figure of the "well-willer" as artist, patron and scholar, is a rudimentary history of connoisseurship running parallel to the history of art and supporting its development at every stage, not only by the well-willer's discerning judgment, "infallible conjecture" about attribution, and true estimation of value, but by a kind of sympathetic participation in the Idea of art itself.

In that history, just as the artist strives for place with those who came before, so the collector stands in a venerable line going back at least to that "most noble *Romane*" propitiously named *Vindex*, who is "highly commended by *Statius Papinius* for his rare judgement in all kinde of Art":

> [W]ho dareth ever strive with Vindex, sayth he, to discerne the old drawings of the Artificers, and to restore his Author unto such statues as have no inscription? He shall shew you what brasse Myron belaboured with a watchful diligence; what marble got life by the carving-iron of the laborious Praxiteles; what ivorie was smoothed by Phydias: what statues doe as yet retaine the breathing infused into them by Polycletus his furnaces; what line doth a farre off confesse the ancient Apelles. (77)

If history asks "*who doth strive with Vindex,*" Junius can answer with his own implied commendation of Arundel: "There are every where in our age also a great many of noble descent and eminent places, who having made an end of their urgent affaires, doe after the example of this same *Vindex* recreate themselves in the contemplation of the divine workes of excellent Artificers" (77). Men like Arundel given to the *vita contemplativa* of art combine the diagnostic skill of the physician (able to tell "*what statues doe as yet retaine the breathing infused into them*") with the discernment of the genealogist (able to see "*what line doth a farre off confesse the ancient Apelles*"). Such an ability to see "*a farre off*" in turn implies a kind of double vision, immediate and historical. To recognize the distinctive style of an Apelles from across the room is, at the same time, to certify that the painting stands legitimately in the line of Apelles.

The subsequent history of art (one thinks of Winckelmann, Berenson, and Warburg as the heirs of Junius, in the line of Vindex) will bear out the same close affiliation of artistic practice, scholarly expertise in identification and authentication, and collecting reflected in the composite figure of Junius's benevolist.

Junius's own career also suggests the importance of philology as the matrix of art history, a connection also stressed by Ellenius in his survey of such contemporaries of Junius in the field of Latin art literature as the French Jesuit Julius Caesar Bulengerus (29).Philology concerns itself with origins and histories, and takes as its purview the same canon of classical texts from which a history of art will be constructed. From the philologist's point of view, moreover, what we have described as Junius's piecing together of a cento—a quilt of classical *sententiae* forming a pattern that reveals, in turn, the "conceived Images" of ancient art—can be thought of as the piece-meal reassembly of a lost language, of art itself as a language with its own structural "parts" akin to those of rhetoric and poetics, and its own history. The commonplaces of the *ut pictura poesis* tradition support this comparison in broad terms, as does Junius's professional facility in translation, whether in his Anglo-Saxon scholarship, or in his turning the Latin text of the *De pictura veterum* first into English and then into Dutch. As the philologist confronting a *visual* language even more fragmentary and obscure than Old English was to Renaissance scholarship, Junius as it were provides a translation based upon the traces of ancient art to be found in the cognate *written* languages of antiquity. Like Vindex of old, he is able "*to restore his Author unto such statues as have no inscription*" by finding the place in the archive where such statues are "inscribed." The same comparison is evident in such passages as that in which Junius uses the example of writing to illustrate the orderly application of color, citing as his authority the noted cento-writer, Gregory of Nazianzus:

> For as all the letters doe not concurre to the writing of every name, but such onely as are proper for it; so doth not the whole multitude of all colours meete to the making of a picture, but some part of them onely, and these not wildly scattered upon a boord, but well and orderly digested by a most accurate and judicious Art: *He is the best Painter,* sayth *Greg. Naziansene, who expresseth in his picture true and breathing shapes; and not he, who vainly mixing many*

> *faire colours representeth nothing else in his worke but a painted tempest.* (272–73)

The "breathing shapes" expressed by the best painters, like the "breathing infused" into the statues cast in Polycletus's furnaces, take on the color and heat of living beings, speaking pictures whose language is as "well and orderly digested" as the most judicious orator's, and so yields up its meanings to the philologist.

In the portraits by Mytens and Van Dyck examined in Chapter 1 (figs. 1and 3) we saw Arundel in his dual role as the founder of a sculpture gallery and the (would-be) founder of a colony, and we examined the connections between the two through the eyes of the painter. What would the reader of *The Painting of the Ancients* add to that description? In a passage that both recalls the practice of epic poets and anticipates Lessing's formulation of the "pregnant moment," Junius writes that, unlike the historiographer, who "discourseth of affaires orderly as they were done," the painter "thrusteth himselfe into the very middest" of an action: "recoursing from thence to the things fore-past, preventing likewise the things to come, he maketh his Art all at once represent things alreadie done, things that are adoing, and things which are as yet to be done" (311). The Van Dyck portrait shows Arundel contemplating the things "yet to be done" in Madagascar while in its representation of his antiquities it reminds us of "the things fore-past" which he has already done, and which predict the success of the future venture. The representation of events is both personal (in that it records Arundel's achievements and reveals his ambitions) and historical (in that, through Arundel, it connects the ancient world with the new). Thus, if Arundel's globe is a *microcosmos* of the world, the span of his career, as suggested in the painting's "recoursing" the past and "preventing" the future, may be seen as a *microchronos* of a grand historical process connecting the reclamation of antiquity with the fulfilment of a colonial destiny.

In the Mytens portrait, the handling of time is no less subtle. Arundel's sculpture gallery is a window onto a past made present. It will strike Junius's reader as the embodiment of a lost world of art which could hitherto only be "conceived" through a welter of literary references. Continuing the project of historical recuperation shadowed in the myth of Isis's search for Osiris, the gallery forms an *ensemble*, in the strong sense: not an assembly of individual pieces merely, but, ideally, the re-assembly of those pieces *magnum in parvo* into the body of classical sculpture itself. To the philologist's eye, furthermore, it is as if the gallery exhibits an array of visible quotations. that, together, bespeak the larger whole. Pieces "wildly scattered" across the ancient world are here "well and orderly digested" in Arundel's gallery, itself a "digest" of classical sculpture. Like the colors applied by the "most accurate and judicious Art" of the painter, or the passages collected and arranged by the scholar, the statues as they appear in (the Mytens painting of) Arundel's gallery are arrayed into a kind of linear syntax, which also allows us (by the "judicious art" of the painter's perspective) to read the sequence 'back' into the depths of the image. This orderly recession of the figures creates a strong sense of their historical distance that plays against the equally strong sense of their immediate presence, just in the next room.

In Junius's history, furthermore, the scholar's job is to reconstruct the hidden recesses of a subject only partly visible in its literary representation. The Mytens portrait engages the viewer in an analogous process. Although parts of the gallery are obscured from sight, the perspectival "rationalization of space," in William Ivins's well-known phrase, makes it possible to form a complete idea of the gallery by counting the number of tiles on the floor and noting the disposition of the visible statues against the architectural detail of the room: for example, the design of the room requires that we imagine two statues that we cannot see, bracketing the near archway, to balance the two we can see bracketing the far archway opening onto the Thames.

In both paintings, the status of the work of art as the collector's *property* draws our attention. Like the globe to which Arundel points in the *Madagascar Portrait*, the gallery towards which he gestures in the Mytens is a little world made cunningly, with Arundel as both guide and proprietor. The *Madagascar Portrait* asks us to view its richly painted detail as the material evidence of the sort of painting Arundel can afford to commission. The sumptuous textures of the sitters' clothing playing off the hard sheen of the globe invokes the painterly finish of a Holbein portrait. What we see elides the patron's ownership of such exquisite objects and his possession of the gorgeous painting in which they are recorded. It also asks us to imagine, with Arundel, what we cannot yet see: the colony which exists, as yet and only until its preciptous collapse, as the paper creation of a joint-stock company under Arundel's sponsorship, and here before us only as a virtual presence "conceived" in and by the painting. The relationship of the visible site of Madagascar Island on the painted globe to the conception of the not-yet-visible colony of Madagascar in the world is congruent, in this viewing, with the relationship between the statues in (Mytens's conception of) Arundel's gallery and the patron's conception of the larger, no-longer-visible Greek and Roman world of which they are the remnant. Whether looking forward or backward, both paintings incorporate far distant times and places into a presence which is not only conceived but, through the power of conception, *possessed.* Both paintings document powerful acts of imaginative appropriation. Just as the artist's storing up of images warrants the collector's storing up of paintings, so the ability to conceive a project carries an implicit right to realize it in the world—or to see its realization in the world as appropriate to the power of conception. Thus, a further congruence is asserted: between the material portrait itself (a "Van Dyck" or a "Mytens"), what it represents (statues, galleries, globes, books), and what it allows us to conceive (future colonies and past cultures), all as valuable possessions. Part of the significance of the Mytens is our awareness, and the artist's, that this portrait will end up hanging in an Arundelian gallery very much like the one it depicts.

Arundel may own the Mytens portrait, but—to recur to the central question of the cento—by what right can he claim to "own" the works of the classical sculptors it represents, let alone (in a more attenuated but nonetheless powerfully implied sense) the whole of antique sculpture of which these examples are a part? How far are we to press the implicit claim in these paintings that imaginative possession confers the right of actual possession? When this question arises in relation to a literary text, it is normally regarded as a question of influence and originality rather than of economics, a reflection of the fact that the writer does not normally claim to *own* the words in his possession in any material sense. If his text accuses him of thievery—crying out against him, "*fur es*"—the predecessor from whom he took the purloined phrase stands under the same indictment, and no one can produce a bill of sale.

Intentionally or not, writing is always the writer's appropriation, but never his property, bought and paid for like the statues in Arundel's gallery. Language is held in common, as a shared commonplace not subject to any writer's enclosure; it is based upon a cornucopian, not a zero-sum economy. The more it is used, the more it increases. Terence Cave writes that the Renaissance text, "in so far as it *is* a mosaic of *topoi*," as it is so conspicuously in Junius or in Du Bellay, whom Cave has in mind, foregrounds "the contrast (or equivalence) between *copia* as plenitude and *copia as copy*" (75). While stricken by the melancholy thought that writing is always rewriting, the "dismembering and reconstruction of what has already been written," the writer can nonetheless be reassured that his efforts only contribute to the copiousness of language as such, and that copying deprives no author of his rights because the copyist makes no claim to them. In the classical metaphor, language is borrowed from a *thesaurus*, or treasure-house, the community stockpile from which anyone may make a withdrawal in time of need, and its very expenditure augments the store from which it was taken. To copy someone else's writing does not diminish his supply; the purchaser can own a copy of the *Aeneid*, but the *Aeneid* "itself" is not for sale. Even in our own day, when writing is subject to the laws of copyright and "intellectual property," the author's "right" to his "own" work expires in time, and the work eventually returns to the public domain. In what contrary sense can Arundel be said to own the objects depicted in the portraits, no less than he does the portraits themselves?

In both portraits, although more obviously in the Mytens, Arundel occupies the formal place of an interlocutory figure, ushering the viewer into the world of the painting and, in this role, mediating the question of "ownership." In the realm of sacred painting from which this convention is taken, the one who stands on the threshold of painting's fictive space is not understood to own the objects in that space. His function is to "speak between" our world and that occupied by the Virgin or the saints, whose experience we are invited to share in an act of communal participation and devotion. Typically, the interlocutor's presence in the painting acknowledges his prior role as the donor—the one whose authority within the image is certified by his having *given it away* at the moment of the commission, even before the image came into being. The generic shift from sacred participation to secular spectatorship in the Mytens portrait also signals a shift in the role of the interlocutor from donor to owner. Arundel's open invitation to the viewer of the Mytens portrait is meaningful only insofar as it claims, and forgoes, the power of exclusion conferred by ownership. Speaking of Arundel's "matchlesse collection of designes," Junius had assured his reader that "our Honourable Lord out of his noble and art-cherishing minde, doth at this present expose these jewells of art to the publike view" (71), an assurance that more than anything else reflects the Earl's *noblesse oblige* in deigning to open his treasures to the the visitor. We are made aware that this is *his* gallery, private property to which we are allowed access only by permission of the owner. At the same time, the Mytens portrait makes us aware that, in a sense, Arundel is excluded from his own gallery. The Earl sits outside the room, on the threshold, capable of entering into an imaginative or even magical relation to "his" possessions symbolized by the (illusory) penetration of staff into the space of the gallery, but separated from "their" world.

One response to this dilemma of ownership is already implied in Junius's conflation of the artist, the "well-willer" of art, and the scholar. In the Knole version of the *Madagascar Portrait* the two figures of Arundel and Junius (if we accept the traditional identification), patron and scholar, are connected formally by being shown in parallel three-quarter view. As we have seen, the painter practices an "accurate" and "judicious" skill which also qualifies him as a critic. By the same token, the "well-willer" bridges the distance to the work by participating in the artist's "idea," by virtue of which his apprehension is full and immediate, not subject to the contingencies of history. Possessing the material, visible object opens a path to the invisible and the ideal. We say that the collector is "possessed by" the idea of the painting. Such inspiration in turn makes the object his own quite apart from whatever funds may have changed hands in the acquisition. Thus, in the Mytens portrait, Arundel's staff seems to give the statue whose base it touches a "true and breathing shape," reviving the spirit imparted to it by its creator and so completing the work of creation begun by the original artificer. In this subtle negotiation of a kind of joint ownership, the centoist's ambiguous labors of re-collecting bits of language that are "his and not his own" is reprised but converted literally into the art collector's asset.

What might otherwise come under suspicion as the misappropriation of antique art—its uprooting and removal from the place of its origin, its commodification and sale, its alien status as an exile in a foreign land—can be conceived instead as a return to its rightful owner, an act of *re*possession. Although the Mytens and the Van Dyck are separated in time by some years, we may also imagine the two paintings as joined in a narrative of reciprocity: Just as the Earl's own destiny might have carried him from Arundel House in the Strand to a distant island possession in Madagascar (to which he seems already transported in thought), so by a kind of compensatory exchange the statues of the ancients have been transported from their homelands where they are were neglected and undervalued to their "rightful" place in Arundel House. In its teleological thrust toward perfection, Junius's history of art supplies the rationale by which we can see Arundel's gallery as *the place,* in an honorific as well as a geographical sense, which the great works of antiquity, however scattered and temporarily forlorn, had always been destined to occupy.

What we have been considering, in effect, in this collaboration of Junius's text, Arundel's gallery, and the portraits by Mytens and Van Dyck, is a founding moment in the institution of the great private art collection in England and America—and, more remotely, of the public art museum that would take its place. Risking a long historical jump, we might observe that every detail of Junius's rhetoric can still be heard after four centuries in contemporary praise for one of Arundel's modern counterparts, Henry Clay Frick, whose collecting habits were just as avid (not to say ruthless) and extravagant as the Earl's. Writing in 1928, nine years after the death of the great industrialist, his hagiographer George Harvey assures us that "Mr. Frick's love or art was innate," and although "he undertook his new avocation with characteristic caution and only after studies as thorough and as painstaking as he ever applied to a business venture, he quickly developed a rare power of discrimination that he applied unhesitatingly" to his acquisitions (George Harvey 331). Harvey goes on to quote at length from a tribute written by one Royal Cortissoz, entitled "A Noble Landmark in our Art History," and published simultaneously with the benefactor's will:

> In giving his house along with his pictures and other beautiful possessions he has done all that a collector could do to send [a] Velasquez [sic] or a Rembrandt or a Gainsborough down to posterity, not as a 'museum specimen' but as a human thing, a work made truly for the delight of mankind. We would be lost without museums, but we are trebly enriched when the museum idea is camouflaged, so to say, by the atmosphere of an individual's home. It is an interesting coincidence that, at the time when the historic interiors of Europe and Great Britain are being broken up as never before, the announcement of the Frick bequest should be made. The old order changeth, giving place to the new. Is the ancient tradition to be revived in the United States, ancestral collections being scattered abroad, only to enter upon a more permanent form of existence on this side of the Atlantic? (Qtd. George Harvey 334).

As a well-willer of art, Frick not only purchases it in bulk, but in that very process endows it with something of his own vitality, transforming a "Velasquez" from a "specimen" to something "human." Through Frick's bequest, the paintings in his possession are "given" a new life. This resurrection of the artist is part of a larger providential drama ("The old order changeth") in which the "ancient tradition," "broken up" and "scattered"—now, the exhausted and bankrupt European tradition, rather than the classical tradition as it was for Arundel and Junius—is to be given a "more permanent form of existence" in America. If Arundel's collection represented a *tranlatio imperii* from the ruins of the ancient world to Britain, Frick's would represent a similar renascence of old world culture "on this side of the Atlantic." And if Arundel House once offered a glimpse of the golden age restored, at the Frick Museum in New York as well as "at Clayton—the Pittsburgh home of industrialist and art collector Henry Clay Frick—the splendor of America's gilded age lives on" (Brochure for The Frick Art & Historical Center, Pittsburgh, qtd. Schreiner 253), in the comfortably domesticated "atmosphere of an individual's home."

At the beginning, we are told, Frick bought pictures "solely for the gratification of himself, his family and his friends." But after viewing the famous Wallace collection in London he was inspired to "make his own as complete and as nearly perfect as possible for ultimate exhibition, suitably housed and amply endowed for acquirement of meritorious additions for all the years to come, to the people of his own country" (George Harvey 332). "'The American people,' [Frick] said, 'are fond—

and properly so—of going to Europe, chiefly to see the famous paintings and other works of art there. I am going to try to bring some of them here where all Americans may have the opportunity of seeing them without crossing the ocean'" (George Harvey 336). At the end, while showing a friend the very last painting he purchased on September 7, 1919, less than three months before his death, he "looked down the long gallery" and remarked quietly: "'I want this collection to be my monument'" (George Harvey 336). Frick's retrospective look "down the long gallery," a look at once opening onto the monuments of the past and glimpsing a future in which the gallery itself will figure in the public eye as a "monument" to its creator, is a deeply conventional gesture in the history of collecting. It returns us, ultimately, to the view of Arundel's gallery in the Mytens painting, with its deep perspective drawing us into the space of the monuments of antiquity, which now stand as a monument to the ambition and public spirit of the collector. Both the careful ordering of the statues in the Mytens painting of Arundel's gallery and Frick's desire to make his own collection as "complete" and "nearly perfect" as possible illustrate one aspect of Susan Stewart's distinction between the souvenir and the collection:

> In contrast to the souvenir, the collection offers example rather than sample, metaphor rather than metonymy. The collection does not displace attention to the past; rather, the past is at the service of the collection.... The collection seeks a form of self enclosure which is possible because of its ahistoricism. The collection replaces history with *classification*, with order beyond the realm of temporality. In the collection, time is not something to be restored to an origin; rather, all time is made simultaneous or synchronous within the collection's world.... While the point of the souvenir may be remembering, or at least the invention of memory, the point of the collection is forgetting—starting again in such a way that a finite number of elements create, by virtue of their combination, an infinite reverie. (150–51)

Stewart's description of the elements of a collection working "in combination toward the creation of a new whole that is the context of the collection itself" (152–53) fits Mytens' image and Frick's imagining of a collection perfect for "ultimate exhibition." As its *own* world, requiring neither a biographical relation to the collector nor an historical relation to its original context, the collection is self-possessed: the history of its acquisition, and thus the ambiguities of ownership, are erased. In compensation, objects take on new meanings in relation to others within the space of their display. While the collection may aspire to "represent" a certain historical moment (Dresden china of the 18th century), historically incoherent juxtapositions (by size, or subject, or color) are no less meaningful within the rules of the collection. And in what sense can a collection, however extensive, be regarded as "complete," or "perfect" except in relation to itself?

Eugenio Donato's observation, offered in an essay on Flaubert's *Bouvard and Pécuchet* and cited by Stewart, that the "set of objects the Museum displays is sustained only by the fiction that they somehow constitute a coherent representational universe" (161), is especially apt for the vast and fantastic collections of Arundel's contemporary, the Emperor Rudolf II, in Prague. From his accession in 1576 until his death in 1612, Rudolf employed his resident artists, craftsmen, and agents in the field—Jacopo Strada, the Emperor's arts administrator, has been called the "Bernard Berenson of the Renaissance" (Trevor-Roper 108)—to amass an unprecedented collection of statuary, paintings, jewelry, mirrors, coins, clocks, optical devices, perpetual motion machines, and rare manuscripts, as well as a botanical garden and a menagerie of wild beasts. His fabled *Wunderkammer* contained, among other bric-a-brac, "two iron nails from Noah's Ark, a jaw of one of the sirens from Homer's *Odyssey*, the horn of a unicorn, and wondrous figures formed by mandrake roots" (Demetz 218). (Not surprisingly, Rudolf's favorite painter was Arcimboldo, whose portraits are themselves bizarre collections of vegetables, or library books, or slabs of meat composed into human faces.)

This Borgesian potpourri was nevertheless conceived as having its own internal order, the fiction of a universe filled with, and bound together by, objects of great magical power. A student of occult correspondences, Rudolf schooled himself in the cosmology of Tycho Brahe and the Hermeticism of Giordano Bruno and John Dee, all in his employ at various times, and perhaps in the Kabbalism of the "the fabulously learned rabbi of Prague, Judah Loew" (Trevor-Roper 101). Recent scholarship has shown that "these collections were not merely a hodgepodge of curiosities but also expressions of a philosophical idea about the universe in which all things and corresponding human affairs had their proper place. The first inventory, as early as 1611, suggested that Rudolf's mind, mortally tired of the chaotic world, found refuge in this private cosmos of precious objects, neatly ordered in categories of *naturalia, artificialia,* and *scientifica"* (Demetz 217).

A less ambitious but similarly heterogeneous cabinet of curiosities was described in 1599 by a Swiss traveler in London, Thomas Platter. The collection of Walter Cope—like Arundel after him, both an antiquarian and a colonial adventurer—contained, *inter alia,* an Indian stone axe, a mummified child, a unicorn's tail, a Chinese box, a trick mirror and a sea mouse (Mullaney 40). For Steven Mullaney, such a collection hangs together as a representation of the "strange," of the "alien, anomalous, dissimilar, barbarous"—in short, of the "Other" (43). It stands apart from the everyday as a world (dis)ordered by a spirit of play and holiday, a world Mullaney will go on to compare to the Shakespearean stage. As such, it figures as an attempt to encapsulate and domesticate the threatening, and to display it in a safe arena (like native Americans in Whitehall) where We, who understand ourselves as not the Other, can observe it at our leisure.

The fact that the self and the other, in this new-historicist construction, can never be walled off, and that Elizabethan culture in various ways on-stage and off always transgresses the boundaries it tries to establish, nonetheless rests on a view of the collection as disinfected of its historical circumstances, the objects it contains "reduced to the status of sheer objects, stripped of cultural and human contexts" (43). The completeness of such collections can only depend upon a principle of exclusion by which everything else in the world that does not fit (into the category of the "strange," for example) cannot be admitted. Collections in this sense make possible the invention of "worlds upon worlds," as Donne says of seafarers' discoveries—empty spaces, utopian nonspaces with no histories, the secluded world of Prospero's secret studies, supplementary worlds free of all contingency, including change and death.

To emphasize the detached, ahistorical self-enclosure of the collection—its (merely) "metaphorical" relation to the original context from which the objects have been taken—foregrounds the "timelessness" that we ascribe to galleries such as Arundel's. Ideally, collections attempt to secure their contents from the vagaries of fortune and the ravages of time, not only by preserving them from deterioration but by sequestering them in a realm from which time itself has been excluded. The temporal self-sufficiency of the collection in this respect, however, slights the possibility of its equally strong connection to history and to memory that Stewart ascribes instead to the "souvenir."

The Renaissance invention of the long gallery for the display of paintings and statuary, with its careful placement of objects in an architectural setting, already embodies a conceptual space which since ancient times had been associated with the *ars memorativa.* For the mnemotechnologist, things are preserved in, and retrieved by, the memory only by being placed into the fixed niches of one's permanent collection of images. Thus, in "The Gallery" (31–33), Andrew Marvell invites his lady to view his soul, which in memory of her has been "Compos'd into one Gallery" and furnished with portraits of her in the various guises (as "an Inhumane Murtheress," as "*Aurora* in the Dawn," as "an Enchantress," and as "*Venus* in her pearly Boat") that have marked the history of their love:

> These Pictures and a thousand more,
> Of Thee, my Gallery dost store;
> In all the Forms thou can'st invent
> Either to please me, or torment:
> For thou alone to people me,
> Art grown a num'rous Colony;
> And a Collection choicer far
> Then or *White-hall's*, or *Mantua's* were. (ll. 41–48)

From our initial view of the first four portaits, the perspective suddenly deepens to reveal "a thousand more" down the length of this mental gallery, which not only surpasses the choicest collections of the age in value and size, but which also suggests, in the conceit of the poet's being "peopled" by her many images, the very comparison that we have seen in the portrait by Van Dyck, between the collection (in Arundel's case of objects recalling the distant past) and the establishment of a distant colony.

Furthermore, the apparent convergence of those objects at an apparently "distant" vanishing point makes such a gallery the model of perspectival vision. In its engagement of the viewers' eye as we look "back" down the length of the room, the gallery becomes an instance of perspective as historical vision, a Panofskian "symbolic form" for history itself. In this sense the gallery is part of the meaning of the collection: indeed, it structures the very possibility of the collection as such having a meaning, one different from, say, that imparted to a collection of photographs arranged on a mantel, or a collection of butterflies displayed in a cabinet. Whether one thinks of such a collection as cut off from its original context, or of opening a perspectival window through which its past may be "seen" at a distance, there is a psychological, if not an etymological, truth in thinking about the "long" gallery (to recur to Stewart) as a "longing" gallery. The "longing" evoked by the collection for a self-sealed world or for a new beginning is matched, as we have seen through Junius's eyes, by a longing for a vanished past recoverable at least, and at most, in pieces; and the figure for this longing for the whole through possession of the part is not metaphor but synecdoche.

The Burtonian melancholy shadowing every portrait of Arundel, or in Rudolf's case the griefs afflicting an imperial mind "mortally tired of the chaotic world," turns the desire to (re)collect the past into an obsessive ritual of mourning that can never be "complete." Typically, of course, collections are also intended to preserve the memory of the collector. *New York* magazine recently reported on a "cabinet of horror" assembled by a retired urologist and containing Lincoln's bloodstained collar, Göring's monogrammed underwear, the bloody seatcover from Kennedy's Dallas limousine, and (appropriately for a urologist), "Napoleon's phallus, severed posthumously by two vengeful Corsican doctors." According to the article, Dr. John Lattimer, now eighty-four and evidently concerned with his own posthumous reputation, would like to put more of these treasures "on public display so that his mark as a collector might be preserved. 'If you die unexpectedly,' he says, 'all of your thoughts go down the drain'" (January 11, 1999, p. 12). Coincidentally, as has just recently come to light, the coffin which first held the body of the assassinated young President was secretly dumped from a plane into the ocean, evidently to prevent its becoming a Kennedy collectible. It must have seemed preferable to those charged with disposing of such relics to sink the coffin down the drain, into an oblivion that would secure it as a memory utterly private to itself, rather than to risk the transfer of its memorial power to some collector.

The losses which the collection is intended to replace may be a very intimate ones. It seems more than coincidental that so many of the great American art collections were—as Martha Sanger writes of her great-grandfather, Frick—"shaped by grief" (19). J.P. Morgan developed "an obsessive need to collect" after his father died in 1890. When Leland Stanford, Jr., an only child, died of typhoid in 1884, at age fifteen, his father established Stanford University as his memorial. Meanwhile his mother, Jane Stanford

> began to construct a museum and collect antiquities. Because young Leland had started his own collection of antiquities and had fashioned two museum rooms on the third floor of his parents' home in San Francisco to display his treasures, Jane dismantled these rooms and had them installed in the heart of the museum.... By 1900, the Leland Stanford Jr. Art Museum was the largest privately owned museum in America. (Sanger 21)

A posthumous portrait displayed in these rooms—a museum within a home, dismantled and reconstructed as a home within the "heart" of a museum—shows the boy who had originally fashioned those two rooms "contemplating Greek ruins" (Sanger 21). We may take these two rooms as the figure for the way in which the museum can stand, in this instance literally, as a *memento mori*.

In her "intimate portrait" of the collector (itself a fat, coffee-table monument to the family legacy), Frick's great-granddaughter argues with some plausibility that many of the paintings Frick acquired over the years, including those he found personally most compelling, contained some reminder of his eldest child, Martha, who died at six in 1891. The steel baron who called in the Pinkertons to break the Homestead Strike emerges in this account as the father ever unconsoled over the death of a beloved child, and ever determined to piece together her lost image by adding to his collection. Frick's final acquisition, the painting that moved him to say, "I want this collection to be my monument," was Vermeer's *Mistress and Maid.* It shows a woman about to receive a note that she regards with apprehension—could it contain the dreaded news of a child's death?—and, on the table before her, a jewel box perhaps recalling, for Frick, the coffin that held the body of the child he thought of as his "jewel" (Sanger 157). No one knows whether it was such associations that moved Frick so to be affected by the painting that he changed his usual seat at the dinner table to have it constantly in view. If so, perhaps the irony was not lost on him that the object acquired at enormous cost (over four million dollars today) held the memory of the one priceless jewel forever beyond his reach.

Painting has always given us images to remind us of the individual dead, whether martyred schoolteachers or treasured children. At the same time, the loss at the heart of the collection may be more profoundly cultural. Patients visiting Freud's apartment at Berggasse found themselves surrounded by the analyst's remarkable collection of antiques from the classical world, Egypt, and Palestine, which, according to Peter Gay, "Toward the end of Freud's life...added up to more than two thousand items, rounded out with a well-thumbed library on archaeology." His patients' attempts during therapy to delve into their own past was appropriately staged in a kind of cultural memory theater, implicitly connecting individual case histories with the religious and mythic substrate of the western mind. In the gallery where Freud collected his case histories, ontogony recapitulates archaeology, as his desk, cabinets, bookshelves, and tabletops were peopled with a "massive display of silent witnesses to ancient civilizations" (Gay 140–41)—a reminder that, in the light of Freud's meditations on Moses and Oedipus, the life of the patient in the Berggasse must understood as part of an extended family history.

If collecting (and recollecting) is a way of preserving or constructing such family histories, the history of art as it passes down to the age of Arundel is itself a kind of family history. As Paul Barolsky has argued in the case of Vasari, who spent a lifetime collecting biographical materials for *The Lives of the Artists*, "The genealogies of noble Florentine houses, modelled on the patriarchy of the Hebrew Bible, are an important model for Vasari's very concept of art history—which is a genealogy of artists both real and imaginary" (10–11). James Heffernan, who cites this passage in a recent discussion of the rhetoric of art criticism, connects Vasari himself as the "father of art history" to the history he writes, which is "essentially the history of families" (23). Vasari's paternal role in relation to "his own" history, like that of the patient to his case history, and the collector to his collection, is doubled in accordance with the precept that the child is father to the man: all three (re)assemble a body of which they are, at once, the progenitors and the descendents—just as Frick both fathers and survives his lost "jewel." Insofar as the collector always stands, in this virtual way, at the "head" of his own collection, his project is inevitably autobiographical, retracing the lineaments of a self concealed in the materials of the collection.

On a broader canvas history painting may also record losses on a much larger and more horrifying scale. In *The Painting of the Ancients*, as an example of "Images of things" that painters will "labor to store up in their Phantasie" as a collection of impressions for future use, Junius offers a detailed account—in effect, an elaborate ekphrasis of the artist's mental image, and the longest such passage in the book—of the "expugnation of a great and populous towne." Here, in what is perhaps the most astonishing description in Caroline literature of the depredations of war visited upon a civilian population, the butcherlike cruelty suffered by Cassianus is writ large as rampant carnage laying waste an entire city:

> [W]hole troupes of armed men, having broake up the citie gates, and thrown downe a good part of the walls, run through the towne after a most tumultuous manner, and cause every where a trepidation like unto a ruine, whilest with sword and fire they do promiscuously destroy things sacred and profane. (69)

Junius goes on for four pages (69–72) to imagine the sounds and sights associated with this promiscuous destruction: the "crackling noise" of the houses being pulled down; the howling of women at the mercy of marauding soldiers who "adde rapes to murders, and murders to rapes"; the sight of "desolate multitudes" falling in heaps or streaming out of the city as refugees or being led off as captives in chains. "You cannot cast your eyes anywhere, but you shall meet with…armed, unarmed, boyes, horses, weapons, men, women, household-stuffe, enemies, citizens, all are mixed together." Panic and confusion reign as people tumble together at the city gates "crowding and striving to get out first: men and horses, wounded and unwounded, living and dead, swords and pikes, bundles also of precious things make all but one heape stopping up the gates." Exile or death are the only alternatives. All coherence gone, the world of the town is, like its hapless defenders, "cut in pieces." Brothers and sisters are "pulled asunder." Aged men and old decayed women are "haled and pulled for meere sport." Any ripe virgin who chances to fall into the hands of the insolent conquerors is "in danger to be torne in pieces by them." In the end, the killing field is described in a sentence all the more stark for the three disjoint phrases that capture both the urgency and the horror of notes scribbled at the scene: "There lie every where scattered upon the bloudy ground all manner of weapo[n]s, dead bodies, whole joynts cut off."

Such scenes were all too common in the Dutch resistance against Spain and again, at the time of Junius's writing, throughout northern Europe during the Thirty Years' War, a calamity that cannot have been far from the mind of a man with Junius's roots in the continent. But this is not any particular city; or rather, it is any city in ruins—the archetypal city, from Troy to Carthage and Rome, to Vienna and Antwerp. Here Junius gives us an image of violence by which everything is dismembered, scattered, torn in pieces: the body of Osiris suffering its tragic *sparagmos* again and again as the leitmotif of secular history. It is as if the artistic remains of those dead cities in antiquity, statues missing arms and legs, were in some ghastly way the petrified form of the violence to which their makers fell victim. Like Erasmus or "Democritus Junior" surveying the folly of humankind, Junius imagines the social body ravaged by "fire and sword" in a scene that magnifies the "butcherlike cruelty" once inflicted on the martyr Cassianus into the way of the world.

Whether Cassianus received a heavenly crown for his suffering Junius does not say. Nor does he speculate, as Donne is wont to do, on the resurrection of the body as the ultimate consolation for earthly suffering. In one sermon perhaps familiar to Junius, Donne imagines that on that glorious day every mutilation will be repaired—it being no impediment to the miraculous power of God to piece together even the unfortunate bicoastal amputee who may have lost "an Arme in the East, and a leg in the West" (*Sermons* III, 109; cited in Carey 220). Donne's concern for the man who seems to have strewn parts of himself all over the map glances obliquely at the devastations of early modern warfare, but he finds his comfort in the hope of a final resuturing of humanity. For Junius, the "good and great maker of this Universe" (3) is invoked at the beginning of book one as the creator of a beautiful universe, and so as Himself the original inspiration of painting. Although (as St. Chrisostom had said) men desire to "imitate the wonders of Nature" by *"endeavor[ing] to set forth a lively similitude of divers visible things"* [4]), there is no corresponding vision at the end of Junius's book in which the diversity of things would be gathered up like the sheaves into a whole. We are left instead with a prospect of things "every where scattered upon the bloudy ground," a doleful labor for Isis, with no providential assistance at hand.

It would be an oversimplification to rush to the historically premature conclusion that, for Junius, the only salvation lies in art, or even that the longing for a lost world only partially fulfilled in the possession of its scattered treasures responds to a loss of religious faith—with the collection as secular reliquary. Still, we note Junius's emphasis in the end on the power of "a certaine kinde of Grace" to unify the "five principall points" of painting observed by the ancients. As we have seen, "Picture," like rhetoric, can be divided for purposes of analysis into its constituent parts: Invention, Proportion, Color, Motion, and Disposition. "Yet did not the ancients think that the perfection of Art consisted in a meete observing of these five points, except the whole worke did breath forth a certain kinde of Grace proceeding out of a decent comelinessse of every point by it self, and out of a mutuall accord of all five" (222). This consummate quality of art cannot be earned, as it were, by works: "This grace is not the worke of a troublesome and scrupulous study," but must be attained (in a way parallel to the joint effect of human effort and divine imputation in a theology of "cooperative" grace) through the "mutuall support of Art and Nature" (334). The tinge of a suffusing Christian grace in the achievement of this "perfection," reminiscent of the social grace that harmonizes the various "parts" of Castiglione's courtier, serves the purpose of reunifying the five "points" of painting into one. Such a "mutuall accord" contains the traces of two narratives deeply imbedded in Junius's text and here brought to symbolic closure. The fragmented social body is reconciled through the practice of an inherently irenic art founded upon harmonizing differences; and the body of ancient art is resurrected, its pieces not merely reconstituted but reanimated into a "whole worke" capable of the breath of life. In this way, the formal analysis of art is itself brought into accord with the long history of its subject—the "painting" of the ancients, dead and dispersed, but now recollected, in one sense in the scholar's text, and in another, in the galleries of his patron.

The importation of a secularized "grace" into the discourse of art coincides with the removal of works of art from churches to private collections. Symptomatic of this trend, and of the resistance it provoked, was Rudolf's unsuccessful attempt, despite all the resources and political influence at his command, to detach Dürer's *Assumption* from the Dominican church in Frankfurt-am-Main, and Lucas van Leyden's *Last Judgment* from a church in Leiden (Trevor-Roper 113). At this pivotal moment in the social history of art, where private collections and ultimately public museums become the new home for sacred imagery, Arundel's role as the interlocutor in the Mytens portrait, directing the attention of the viewer to the sculpture gallery beyond, carries something of the resonance of sacred painting, however "pagan" the contents of the gallery itself. The pseudo-sacralization of art implied in this complex gesture claims to redeem the painting of the ancients, even as it registers the loss of the sacred subject once revealed in such scenes, for which these stony marbles stand as a monument. Junius's advice that the painter should "store up" such scenes as that of the ravaged town implies a similar redemptive power, for no matter how terrible the destruction, the town remains in the painter's imagination ready to be reproduced whole—all the mangled parts restored through the grace of art. And yet we know from the history of ekphrastic writing, beginning with the impossibly detailed description of Achilles's shield in Homer, that no painting could possibly contain all the detail and helter-skelter confusion of Junius's passage.

Very near the end of Junius's book, we are given a glimpse of a kind of mini-apocalypse that images both the power and the limitation of art to carry the force of the sacred:

> *Theon*, a most famous Painter, having made the picture of an armed man who seemed to runne most seriously on his enemies that depopulated the country round about, he did thinke it good not to propound [i.e., show] the picture before he had provided a trumpeter to sound an alarme somewhere hard by; the trumpet therefore being heard, the picture was likewise brought forth suddenly at the same instant. *The sound of the trumpet,* sayth *Aelian, possessed the phantasies of the spectators with a more lively impression of a man desperately sallying out to ayd his countrey.* (345)

The "armed man," a surrogate for the painter himself in the desire to make good the losses inflicted by such enemies as we have seen above, will not be permitted to run silently into battle. The revelation of the picture "brought forth suddenly" is accompanied by the "dreadfull noise" of the trumpet (345). In turn, the connection between the modern collector and Theon the ancient painter is strengthened by Junius's odd choice of the word "propound" as the English translation of his Latin original: *proponere*, to "put forward" or to "set forth," in the sense of putting a picture on view. Collectors, as we have seen, will exercise the faculties of a painter when (like Mytens carrying out Arundel's commission) they "imagine well-hung chambers and well-furnished galleries," thus "propounding themselves hereafter an innoxious and a happie life" (82).

To "propound," or advance, an argument, in Junius's Latinate cast of mind, is the same as to set an image before the viewer—a small but significant confirmation at the level of language of the alliance between rhetoric and painting on which Junius bases much of his exposition. Junius uses both words synonymously in the opening Argument: "*My purpose is, by Gods asistance, to set forth the* Art of Painting, *as in old times it hath begun.... The second booke propoundeth diverse means tending to the advancement of this Art. The third book speaketh of the maine grounds of Art, the which being well observed by the old Artificers, made them come neerer to the heigth of perfection"* (1–2). To "set forth" the art of painting is not merely to follow the narrative of its beginning, advancement, and perfection, but to display a "more lively impression" of it by revealing the glorified body of painting interred in its literary history.The narrative recalls a beginning in which the "maker of this Universe" spoke a cosmos into being that was called "by the name of an *Ornament*" (3), and anticipates an endtime in which the perfection of all things will be revealed by the opening (and closing) of a book—and heralded by the "sound of the [last] trumpet." In this history within a history, the example of Theon itself propounds the bond between the revelation of a pagan painting and the final revelation of Christian truth: from this providential point of view, both partake of the "same instant," and the trumpet that sounds in the one resounds in the other.

At the same time, Junius's reader senses the gaps that cannot be bridged even by such strenuous attempts at connection. Theon's painting no longer exists except in its echo, as it were, in Aelian's verbal report

In this painting which cannot be seen at all, the armed man will forever run at his enemies without closing with them. The painting itself, as the painter insists in Aelian's account, could not be shown unless the trumpet sounded to create "a more lively impression" in the viewer than the image alone was able to produce. These ironies shadow Junius's book. They do not dispel the lively impression of the art of antiquity that he himself hopes to propound in *The Painting of the Ancients*, but they create a chiaroscuro effect. The hope was "to collect the lessons of the Ancients, which are now, as it were, severed from the body of the theory of art and bit by bit dispersed among the literary remains of Classical Antiquity, and to arrange the pieces in such a way as to arrive at the contours of true art." Collecting and arranging the pieces cannot reattach the severed limbs of the body of art until the last trumpet blows to signal the victory of *the* Most Famous Painter against His enemies. Until then, and from the time of its invention in Junius's period, art collecting will serve as a vehicle of cultural as well as personal mourning. It is a part of the logic of this process, and no mere accident, that paintings will pass from one collection to another on the death of the collector, or rather into many collections, like a body dispersed bit by bit, on the auction block. In both senses of the word, collection is always recollection.

For Arundel—whose collections would meet with the same fate after his death—the passion for collecting seemed to grow, even as his own fortunes and those of his party waned, through the 1630s and into the 1640s. In such times assembling and cataloguing paintings and antiquities becomes at least a temporary stay against confusion, a little world made cunningly. As we have seen, the *Madagascar* portrait of 1639 reinforces Arundel's authority as the propounder of a colonial venture by including objects that remind us of his collections, as if his dominion over the ancient world were now to be transferred to the new. Like the trumpet heralding Theon's picture, these images of things long unseen until unearthed by the collector give us a livelier impression of the project to be: a colonial plantation not yet visible, but to be founded before long on a distant island. Of this new world, Arundel is the prophet, the seer in whose mind the vision has already taken shape.

As Donne says at the end of the second *Anniversarie*, invoking the traditional figure of Christian preaching at the moment when his anatomy of the old world gives way to a vision of the new illuminated by the memory of Elizabeth Drury, "I am The / Trumpet, at whose voyce the people came" (266, ll. 527–28). In the light of *The Painting of the Ancients*, the moment recorded by Van Dyck in the Madagascar portrait can be seen as pivotal, both in Arundel's career (as he was able to hope, fleetingly, in that year), and more broadly for the culture of the Arundel circle. The center of the painting is occupied by the globe; the remains of antiquity, significant as they are to the symbolism of the painting, have been relegated to the margin. It is as if the painting registers the moment just after the patron has turned *from* his antiquities *to* the calling that will now feed his imagination, and be fed by his coffers. The portrait that might have been, perhaps an "Arundel Contemplating the Bust of Homer," shadows the image like a faint recollection, now supplanted by the present image of Arundel contemplating the island of Madagascar, in anticipation of the colony to spring up there. At this Janus-like moment, Arundel's, and the viewer's, connection to the temporality of things is detached from its anchorage in the past and projected into a future which (like the ancient culture it leaves behind) can be propounded but not possessed. From yet another point of view, we might also see the Van Dyck portrait as implying two other sorts of connection between the old world and the new: a bond of "sympathy" forged through the healing power of Arundel's imagination on the dismembered body of history, and a model of cultural interchange between antiquity and futurity founded on the discovery by William Harvey, Arundel's personal physician, of the "circulatory" system.

4. The Arts of Sympathy: Harvey, Digby and the Arundel Circle

As every science student knows, William Harvey secured his place in the history of medicine for discovering the circulation of the blood. Less known generally, but still studied in detail by historians of early modern science like Walter Pagel, is Harvey's relationship to the medical traditions of his time, chiefly those of the Galenists, the Aristotelians, and, latterly, the Paracelsians. Charles Webster has placed Harvey in his professional context of his day as an influential—ultimately revered—member of the College of Physicians of London in its competition with the barber-surgeons, the apothecaries, and various unlicensed practitioners, none of whom lacked for patients in a plague-ridden age. There has, however, been hardly any attention paid to the broader cultural influence of Harvey's work in the context of the intellectual and artistic passions of the Arundel circle to which, as the Earl's physician and client, he also belonged. Through Junius we have already drawn out one thread connecting the powers of the physician and the collector who, as he examines the body of ancient art, can detect which statues "*as yet retaine the breathing infused into them*" by their creator. In a broader perspective, if the Copernican and Galilean revolutions heralded a "breaking of the circle" in cosmology, Harvey's physiological revolution may be said to have reconstituted it, although on different grounds—by drawing a figure of circulation in the body, proposing the body itself *magnum in parvo* as the model of a circulatory system, and thus providing a resonant figure of thought in politics, antiquities, and geographical exploration as well as in medicine.

Unlike "circulation," the word "sympathy," in the sense of an attraction or mutual response between two separate bodies, has lost virtually all its seventeenth-century meaning as a medical term of art; and unlike Harvey's name, that of Sir Kenelm Digby is generally known only to specialists in Stuart culture. But this medical amateur, promoter of the fabulous "Powder of Sympathy," was no less celebrated than Dr. Harvey in the court world of the 1630s, and he came to enjoy an even more colorful and eccentric literary afterlife, albeit as something of crackpot-savant. One curious fact to be accounted for in the unlikely juxtaposition of these two careers is that, while Harvey's findings were initially met with skepticism, Digby's bogus "sympathetic" cure-all, touted for its power to heal even at a distance from the patient, was widely regarded as possessing an extraordinary medicinal virtue. Indeed, as we shall see, at a crucial point in his own research Harvey himself fell back on a sympathetic explanation of the origin of life. The relation of Digby and Harvey allows us to root the New Historicist figure of cultural "circulation"—which so far as I know has never considered the importance of Harvey as the "Fam'd *Circulator*"—on more solid historical ground, as well as to define the "sympathetic" influence between Arundel and the world of ancient art.

Digby had been already been hailed as a hero in 1628, at the age of twenty-five, for defeating a Venetian fleet at the Battle of Scanderoon while leading a privateering expedition in the Mediterranean. That same year—the year in which Harvey, then fifty, published his findings on the heart—Digby found time to compose his "Observations" on Spenser's *Faerie Queene* In the chapter "Of Antiquities" added to the 1634 edition of *The Compleat Gentleman*, Henry Peacham reserves a special note of praise for Digby in the midst of his encomium on the Earl of Arundel. For when it came to assembling the royal collections, a project inspired by the example of Arundel's "noble Patronage of Arts and ancient learning," Peacham reports that "some of the Old-greeke-marble-bases, columnes, and altars were brought from the ruines of *Apollo's* Temple at *Delos* by that noble and absolutely compleat Gentleman, *Sir Kenelm Digby* Knight" (107–08). Exemplifying Peacham's ideal gentleman, the "compleat" Digby was thus assembled, like the collections in which he had a hand, of many parts: soldier, diplomat, importer of antiquities, literary critic, courtier in the entourage of Queen Henrietta Maria, and himself a patron of the arts, especially of Van Dyck.

In a 1632 family portrait of Digby with his wife, Venetia, and his children, Van Dyck places an armillary sphere at Sir Kenelm's right elbow to suggest the sitter's interest in natural philosophy and navigation. Digby sat for Van Dyck again that year or the next (Sumner 74, 79) for his portrait with a sunflower, the very detail included by the same painter in his own most intriguing self-portrait, and one for which many explanations have been proposed. Given the heliotropic urges of this particular flower, Van Dyck seems to suggest a sympathetic link between the sunflower and its human companion in each portrait, as well as between himself and Digby, the two joined in their desire for fame, perhaps, or as some think, for the illumination of arcane wisdom (Petersson 98–99). As Christopher Brown notes in his discussion of this painting (147), the sunflower could allude as well to Digby's service at court: *The Mirror of Majestie* (1618) compares the courtier to a heliotrope, "waiting upon the sonne of Majestie."

Lady Venetia Digby was found dead one morning in 1633, and—in a gesture that did not quite allay the suspicion that with a husband so proficient in physic, the wife may not have died of natural causes—Sir Kenelm summoned Van Dyck to her chamber to paint an extraordinary portrait of her on her deathbed (fig. 9). Ben Jonson had already written an epigram in praise of Digby (*Underwood* LXXVIII). Now he lavished a ten-part *Eupheme* on the occasion of Lady Venetia's death (*Underwood* LXXXIV) asserting, characteristically, that no painter, but only the poet, can show the Lady's mind. Remarkably, the portrait captures the face of death even as it seems to suggest that the lady is merely asleep and could be awakened by a touch—or by her turning toward the morning sun, which strongly illuminates her face and the bedclothes. When Sir Kenelm was subsequently honored in 1636 by his inclusion in the *Iconography*, Van Dyck's engraved gallery of modern worthies, the motto supplied by Junius for this publication adapts a line from Horace as a comment on Digby's strength in adversity: *Si fractus illabatur orbis intrepedum ferient ruinae*, "If the heavens crack and fall, their ruins will rain down on an unbowed head" (Brown 147).

Diverse titles reflecting a life-long interest in medicine appear under Digby's name, including his *Observations* on Browne's *Religio Medici* in 1644, and a treatise on the vegetation of plants in 1661. His *Choice and Experimental Receipts in Physick and Chirurgery* and *A Choice Col-*

lection of Rare Secrets and Experiments in Philosophy, were published posthumously in 1668 and 1682. By far the best known was A *Late discourse…touching the cure of wounds by the powder of sympathy*. Based on Digby's lecture on this subject at Montpelier in 1657 and translated from Digby's French, the book went through four English editions between 1658 and 1664. The "Powder of Sympathy" held the rarest secret associated with Digby's name, both during the Caroline years in England when he advocated its use, then across Europe after the publication of his book, which went through twenty-nine editions in French, German, Dutch, and Latin as well as in English (Petersson 264).

Digby's powder, with its dubious ability to effect cures at a distance by the action of "sympathy," is arguably the most intriguing if also one of the most preposterous of Renaissance nostrums. It will be the strategy of this chapter, moving between Harvey and Digby, to connect the pioneer of modern physiology to the evident quack. This is a line seldom drawn in the history of medicine, although no one familiar with early modern science will be surprised at the co-existence, and even the cross-pollination, of such contrary pursuits—of what from our point of view looks like serious inquiry and what has been forgotten or repressed as mere magic and superstition. In the context of a broader cultural and literary history of the period, we should not wonder that the "Powder of Sympathy," in contrast to the true advancement of learning represented by Harvey's *De motu cordis*, should have been taken seriously. Most of the salves and potions in the Renaissance pharmacopoeia likely had no more therapeutic value than Digby's powder. Rather we need to ask what underlying and only partly articulated needs should have fed the desire to believe that this cure could work as Digby claimed; we need to find the source of its appeal to the imagination and to specify the network of assumptions in which such nonsense made sense in the age of Arundel.

That appeal is best glimpsed in the enduring fascination of Digby's sympathetic theories. The older meaning of the term, now virtually obsolete, appears most notably in the stirrings felt by Milton's Sin, who, though far from the scene of the Fall, nevertheless responds to Satan's triumph by "sympathy, or some connatural force / Powerful at greatest distance to unite / With secret amity things of like kind / By secretest conveyance" (*Paradise Lost* 10:246–249). Among the references to his work in the medical literature of the 17th and 18th centuries, Digby is cited several times by Cotton Mather in *The Angel of Bethesda*, a manuscript compilation of remedies including, on Digby's authority, a stomach plaster of mithridate and nutmeg (196, 198), and a recipe for ear drops made of rendered eel fat, spirits of wine, and the juice of onions and leeks, by which wonderful cures for deafness have been effected (163).

Digby makes his most recent literary appearance in Umberto Eco's nove *The Island of the Day Before* (1994), in which an entire chapter is devoted to a "A Discourse on the Powder of Sympathy" (Chapter 16). Eco's seventeenth-century hero, Roberto della Griva, reports having met an Englishman known in the salons of Paris as "Monsieur d'Igby" (161). In the incident Eco has him recall, Roberto becomes a (fictional) character inserted into the very vignette about the healing of an accidental sword cut that (the historical) Digby offers as the centerpiece of his own treatise on this marvelous nostrum—a treatise first delivered in 1657 as a "discourse made in a solemne assembly of nobles and learned men at Montpellier in France" (title page) and published the following year.

In this *Discourse*, the nonfictional Digby claims that long before, evidently in the 1620s, experiments conducted by him using this powder were observed with admiration by King James, Prince Charles, and the Duke of Buckingham, and that Bacon, had he lived, planned to include an account of it as an appendix to his natural history (5). For Digby, the efficacy of his preparation—based on an extract of vitriol that might indeed have had some mild antiseptic effect if directly applied to a wound—was convincingly demonstrated at the time a friend named James Howell suffered a deep sword cut on the hand. When, after some days, the wound was no better and in danger of festering, Digby reports that he removed Howell's blood-stained bandage and soaked it a solution of the Powder of Sympathy—whereupon the patient exclaimed that his hand felt instantly cooler and free of pain. The experiment was further confirmed when, out of Howell's presence (the patient had in fact returned home), Digby took the bandage from the solution and hung it before the fire to dry. Back came word from Howell by way of his servant that the injured hand had again become suddenly and painfully inflamed.

Not coincidentally for the argument of this chapter, Eco's fictionalized Digby is conjured up from a vantage point on the edge of European colonial expansion. Roberto della Griva recalls his adventures with "Monsieur D'Igby" while he is lost somewhere in the South Pacific after a shipwreck. Digby's sympathetic cure, displaying a remarkable cultural shelf life, survives under unexpected conditions in far-flung regions. In this association between the Powder of Sympathy and the distant corners of the earth lies an imaginative logic, for the burden of Digby's book is to explain how his amazing powder works at a distance from the patient, extending its healing influence to the sufferer—as Digby proved, to his own satisfaction—from across a room or even from another house. And if from another house, why not from greater distances, even from miles away? That thought lay behind Samuel Butler's sendup of Digby in *Hudibras* as the brave knight Orsin:

> Learned he was in med'c'nal lore,
> For by his side a pouch he wore,
> Replete with strange hermetic powder,
> That wounds nine miles, point blank wou'd solder.
> (III.ii.1029–32)

The problem Digby addresses, and the reason for his inclusion here, has to do with this very power to act at a distance—the same power, on a broader scale, that drives the colonial enterprise.

To compare great things with small, the connection between geographical distances on the map of European expansion and the therapeutic distance from which the Powder of Sympathy exerts its influence is suggested by Digby's claim that he learned the recipe for the powder, as he confides to us, from "a religious *Carmelite* that came from the *Indies* to *Florence*, [who] had also been at *China*" (11). Having imparted to Digby this "secret he had learnt in the Oriental parts," the itinerant Carmelite completes his circle by returning to Persia, thus leaving the author as the sole possessor of an invaluable fragment of arcane wisdom from the East. What cures from afar comes from afar, enabling the possessor to act "sympathetically" on the afflicted just as the religious orders represented by the Carmelite acted upon the denizens of the regions from which the secret comes, offering a ministry compounded of healing balm and invisible distant control.

In the history of Digby's "cure," a logic beyond mere coincidence connects the therapeutic distance covered by the Powder of Sympathy and the global distances covered by the voyager and the colonist. In 1687, one participant in the then-vexing search for an exact method of determining a vessel's longitude at sea proposed a novel application of Digby's powder to this problem in navigation. Dava Sobel's account of this unique proposal in her recent book on longitude needs no elaboration:

> Send aboard a wounded dog as a ship sets sail. Leave ashore a trusted individual to dip the dog's bandage into the sympathy solution every day at noon. The dog would perforce yelp in reaction, and thereby provide the captain a time cue. The dog's cry would mean, "the Sun is upon the Meridian in London." The captain could then compare that hour to the local time on ship and figure the longitude accordingly. One had to hope, of course, that the powder really held the power to be felt many thousand leagues over the sea, and yet—and this is very important—fail to heal the telltale wound over the course of several months. (Some historians suggest that the dog might have had to be injured more than once on a major voyage.) (42)

Whether any dog was ever so recruited to serve the advancement of science is not recorded, but the proposal itself is evidence of Digby's influence—of a "powerful appeal" that was, as his biographer Richard Petersson observes, both "medieval and modern" (275).

The "wounded dog" method for fixing longitude answers to a growing need for real-time communication beyond the power of early modern technology to provide, but capable of being imagined even in such an absurd form. In a Baconian spirit of cooperative investigation, Digby was assiduous in his medical researches, generous in sharing what he dug up, and in France after his relocation there during the Protectorate he was noted for personally treating several difficult cases. Under his care, the Archbishop of Liege and Henrietta Maria's chaplain, Christopher Davenport, recovered from the quartan ague—in both cases, Peterson reports, after "the eminent physician and chemist Van Helmont had given up hope" (259). The "medieval" side of his medical practice is reflected in the miscellany of cure-alls, salves, and potions such as those known to Cotton Mather. These were collected and published after Digby's death by George Hartman as the *Choice and Experimented Receipts of Physick and Chirurgery* (1668). The result was a "bagful of wonder…no less fantastic, no less unorthodox, and no less a mixture of wisdom and foolishness than the rest" of this genre (Petersson 260). The compilation was (medievally) unorthodox in the bizarre ingredients its "receipts" frequently called for (the fat of a boar killed in the act of procreation), but also in its (modern) willingness to flout medical orthodoxies of any kind, Galenic or Paracelsian, to find cures that worked, or were reputed to work, by experience.

It was also medieval in two other senses. In the longest historical perspective, it belongs to a tradition of "sympathetic" cures going back at least to Pliny, preserved through the course of medieval science, and avidly revived as a subject of debate and speculation by the Paracelsians and Rosicrucians, by Van Helmont, and in England by Bacon his *Natural History*. Robert Fludd championed of one variant of such sympathetic therapies, the "weapons-salve," which, when applied to the edge of a blade, would cure the wound that blade had caused (Debus). However, in a looser sense, and from a more skeptical angle, Digby's enthusiasms also seem hopelessly medieval in their credulity. The examples of sympathetic influence educed by Digby in his 1657 address at Montpellier—we do not know with what reaction from the audience in this most sophisticated center of medical education in northern Europe—include the following, all cited without a trace of any irony that might suggest Digby regards these instances as anything other than hard evidence proving his case.Those familiar with the workings of sympathy will have heard of the pregnant woman "brought to bed of a prodigious monstre, exactly resembling an Ape, [on] which she took pleasure to look during the time when she was with child" (108). Similar stories of marvelous births abounded, and all were to be explained as the effects of sympathy: that of the Ethiopian queen who gave birth to a white child because a picture of the blessed Virgin hung over her bed, or of another baby born covered with hair because his mother's taste in art for the bedchamber ran toward a portrait of John the Bapist in his camel's hair coat (186–189). Yet even the knowledgeable may be surprised to learn that venison pasties preserved in pots smell "very rank, and very much changed, having a stronger taste, when the living beasts of the same kind are in rut" (79). Or that those afflicted with foul breath may find a cure in holding "their mouths open at the mouth of a Privy, as long as they can," the "greater stink of the privy drawing unto it, and carrying away the lesse, which is that of the mouth" (76). Or that a certain housewife relied on a knowledge of sympathy to have her revenge on some nasty boys who defecated on her doorstep as a prank and then ran off; by plunging a red hot shovel into the offending pile, she caused the boys to be struck down at that very instant by a searing inflammation in their bowels (127).

What is, however, strikingly "modern" about the use of all of these examples, including that of the healing of James Howell's cut on which the main claim for the "Powder of Sympathy" rests, is Digby's insistence on demonstrating that however improbable they may appear at first sight, these apparent wonders can each be completely explained on natural and material grounds through an understanding of the action of "atoms." With this strategy, Digby's argument does not discard the preposterous in the interest of a new science but rather labors to rationalize and justify it by the most assiduous application of neo-Democratean atomic theory. It is an exercise in demystification which nonetheless preserves something of the mystery of an older world interconnected by the bonds of sympathy that a more skeptical atomic physics—one envisaging, in Donne's words in the "First Anniversary," a world "crumbled out again unto its atomies"—would seem in theory obliged to dissolve.

Thus Digby insists that all of these effects arise from a "material and corporeal participation" (85). There is nothing insubstantial or merely "imaginary" even about such a case as that of a pregnant woman who, having imagined some mulberries, gave birth to a daughter with a mulberry mark on her face. Rather, subtle atoms exuded from real mulberries impressed themselves on the woman's mind to create "like" images of mulberries, which in turn impressed themselves on the face of her unborn child. Similarly, the sympathetic power of the privy cures bad breath by drawing the foul-smelling atoms out of the mouth of the patient toward its own more potent foulness. So, too, the heat atoms from the vengeful woman's spade would have been carried on vagrant atoms from the boys' feces back to their source in the bodies of the boys. Nor is there any charm or magic involved in the alleviation of Howell's suffering by the action of the Powder of Sympathy on his injured hand. The distance between the hand and the basin of water in which the Powder is dissolved is not empty. As Digby explains earlier in the treatise, it is a fundamental tenet of his materialism that the air is already filled with light, which however attenuated and translucent is nonetheless a "corporeal substance," a sea of atoms whose agitation we can feel when the wind blows (34). We recall that the bloody bandage is soaking in the basin of water. Atoms of Howell's blood thrown free of this solution but bathed in its healing vitriol sail across the sea of light back to their source in Howell's cut, thus transporting the medicine directly to the wound (41).

In his defense of the efficacy of his Powder, Digby wants to preserve above all a view of the world in which secret sympathetic connections are possible, a world in which things are held together and work their influence upon each other and yearn to return to their source—like Marvell's neoplatonic drop of dew—when separated from it. But he must now secure this vision on a material basis if it is to be credible. His corporeal explanation makes possible the persistence of old forms shored up by new (or in the case of Digby's atomism, newly refashioned) explanatory mechanisms. Sympathetic cures are unmiraculously effected by the invisible but ordinary action of atoms. It is a remarkable, and remarkably clear, instance of an elaborately concocted, plausible rationalization for the implausible—or rather, for a world that seemed increasingly implausible but could not admitted to be so. Because the examples he gives are (to us) absurd on their face, the strain in Digby's thinking clearly betrays the need to save them from ridicule: what the Powder finally heals is not the wound in Howell's hand but a rent in the network of things that could not be bandaged over by any other means.

It is important to recognize in this theory of influence, as it may be termed, our own critical investment in Digby's powder. An understanding of the bond of sympathy not only helps to explain the connections between things in the world of Digby's imagination—of berries to berry spots on the skin of an infant, or of the venison carcass in the larder to the deer rutting in the field. It also recovers an historically situated figure for the unseen connections among a cluster of texts, images, and cultural projects in the little world we are calling the Arundel circle—for example, the connections to be explored below among Digby's "sympathy," Harvey's "circulation" of the blood, and other forms of commercial and artistic "circulation" as the antiquities trade and the global expansion of empire. Such commonalities must now be reconstituted by acts of sympathetic criticism that find in one text the influence of another even over the distances that separate them. That they are not now apparent but must be brought to view by acts of critical sympathy is due in part to the discrediting of sympathy in which Digby's *Discourse* plays a key role despite its own intentions.

Of these two terms, "sympathy" and "circulation," the latter has the greater critical currency just at the moment when we speak of the dynamics of early modern culture, but both were familiar in Arundel's day as figures of the fundamental connectedness of things, and of patterns of movement describing their interrelation. Although I am mainly concerned with recovering the meaning of "sympathy," I would also take the related term "circulation" into view, although regarded in a more specific historical setting than it usually is when invoked in new-historicist studies. An understanding of the significance of Harvey's work must take account of a long and complex history—masterfully surveyed by Walter Pagel (pp. 89–127)—of allegorical, philosophical, and mystical, as well as strictly anatomical, speculations on circular movements within the body in relation to the circular movements of heaven and earth.

For us, Harvey's *De motu cordis* represents a significant departure from this history by specifying for the first time the exact physiological route by which the blood circulates through the body, thus reconceptualizing the functional connections among the heart and the arterial and venous systems. But without such precedents, Harvey would be less likely to have had the model of a circulatory system in mind as he conducted his investigations. Aquinas had argued on the analogy of the circular motion of the heavens that the heart has its own motion "*non circularem, sed similem circulare conpositum*" ["not circular but like a circular motion] in its pulsations (qtd. Pagel 91). Leo Hebraecus had been "impressed by the similarity of the heart to the...*primum mobile*, because it freely bestows uniform, regular and *circular* (*orbicularem*) motion on all the others," preserving all the bodies in the universe as the heart regulates and preserves the body of man (Pagel 93). In Shakespeare's time Giordano Bruno writes that the spiritual life force ("*virtus, quam spiritualem appelant*") permeating the universe is "effused from the heart into the whole of the body and (flows back) from the latter to the heart, as it were from the centre to the periphery and from the periphery to the centre, following the pattern of a circle" (qtd in Pagel 104).

Again in the generation before Harvey, to take one further example of this tradition, the pioneering student of magnetism John Gilbert wrote a treatise *De mundo* in which he argued from the premise of a universal soul that the earth has a kind of organ system like that of men and animals. As Charles Webster paraphrases Gilbert's scheme, there is "a *circulation* of the humors between the viscera of the earth, in which the humors are carried to the surface in the veins, poured out through springs, and returned to the interior by gravitation" (Bylebyl 16). The topos of the world as a body has its counterpart in that of the body as a "little world" with its own interior routs of circumnavigation. Connecting the two, Donne imagines his physicians "grown / Cosmographers" and examining him on his deathbed as they would a map: like Magellan, he is about to undertake his last journey of "discovery / *Per fretum febris*," through the "straits" of fever to his death in the west ("Hymn to God my God, in my Sickness").

The familiar new-historicist paradigm of the "circulation" of "social energy" needs to be more firmly grounded in what the Renaissance would say actually circulates, and in doing so, serves as a model for social activity: heavenly spheres in the macrocosm, winds and waters in the geocosm and—after 1628—blood in the little world of the human body. What is new here is not the idea of circulation itself or the imagined congruence between circular patterns in the microcosm and the macrocosm. The fact that before Harvey's discovery the heart was long thought to participate in some sort of circular motion by analogy to the general circulation of things testifies to the strength of those analogies, which linked the heavens, the earth and the body. But even if a pioneering natural philosopher like Gilbert, elaborating the same Orphic and Hermetic images of a general circulation that one finds in Dee and Bruno, is said to pave the way for Harvey—and even if such arcane speculations would continue to have their devotees long after Harvey—there is little to nourish them in the dry light of Harvey's careful dissections of the heart. Indeed, with Harvey we stand just at the moment when those patterns are threatened by a weakening belief in overarching systems of analogies, a Baconian skepticism about imposing on the world such aesthetically satisfying, but for that reason, all the more delusively seductive, models of order. The moon was no longer a crystalline sphere but, as the telescope revealed, a jagged and pock-marked rock. The planets wobbled in their elliptical orbits, all coherence gone. Harvey's circulatory theory gained its authority not only by its basis in experimental science, but by its having incorporated and superseded the older, fading images of universal circulation.

What Harvey provides at this very moment of need is a new and powerful image of circulation mapped in the body and demonstrable by the same scientific exactitude by which Digby had thought to demonstrate the efficacy of his mysterious powder. Some physicians were not to be convinced of the circulation of the blood even in the presence of Harvey's own anatomical demonstrations. Others, then as now, resisted the novelty of a discovery that seemed to overthrow received opinion. In Nuremberg with Arundel's diplomatic party in 1636, Harvey is said to have stalked out of the anatomy theater in a rage after one opponent of his theory, the pontifical teacher Caspar Hofmann, remained obdurate. What Hofmann could not, or would not, see is that under Harvey's scalpel the idea of a universally ordered circulation is not discarded but transformed and even reinvigorated—no longer, to be sure, as the manifestation of a system of metaphysical correspondences, but as a discrete bodily "pathway" through which the blood moves with the pulsations of life itself: "A new pathway for the blood must therefore be prepared and thrown open, and being once exposed, no further difficulty will, I believe, be experienced by anyone in admitting what I have already proposed in regard to the pulse of the heart and arteries, viz., the passage of the blood from the veins to the arteries, and its distribution to the whole of the body by means of these vessels" (*De motu* 38–39).

As Digby rationalizes and materializes the workings of "sympathy" by imagining a pathway of blood atoms, a kind of tranlucent sea connecting the soaking bandage and the distant wound, Harvey specifies the idea of bodily circulation by opening a "passage" between the arterial and venous systems for the flow of blood (moving in "vessels," coincidentally) to unite the most distant points in the body with the heart. That Digby's discovery is fantastical and Harvey's the cornerstone of modern physiology should not keep us from noticing that they follow a similar procedure.

Once he has established the structure of the circulatory system on this new basis, Harvey himself feels free to reinvoke the old correspondences, but with a difference:

> I began to think whether there might not be a MOTION, AS IT WERE, IN A CIRCLE. Now, that the blood, forced by the action of the left ventricle into the arteries, was distributed to the body at large, and its several parts, in the same manner as it is sent through the lungs, impelled by the right ventricle into the pulmonary artery, and that it then passed through the veins and along the vena cava, and so round to the left ventricle in the manner already indicated. This motion we may be allowed to call circular, in the same way as Aristotle says that the air and the rain emulate the circular motion of the superior bodies; for the moist earth, warmed by the sun, evaporates; the vapours drawn upwards are condensed, and descending in the form of rain, moisten the earth again. By this arrangement are generations of living things produced; and in like manner are tempests and meteors engendered by the circular motion, and by the approach and recession of the sun" (*De motu* 51).

The abrupt shift in Harvey's account from the mechanics of blood flow to an animist view, given on Aristotle's authority, of the "air and the rain" emulating the movement of the heavenly bodies shows the seam in his work between older and newer discourses of circulation. The thread Harvey draws out of the older texts into greater prominence in his own is the sense of motion: the blood is not simply contained within a circular form but moved under pressure: "forced," "distributed," "impelled," and "passed."

Classical physiology had thought of the blood primarily in its systematic relation to the other three humors rather than in terms of its movement through the body. Harvey, a vivisectionist, is aware of the astonishing force with which blood spurts from a severed artery. Indeed his measurements of the sheer volume of blood flowing through these vessels, all in the same direction, convinced him from the start that bodily circulation could not involve a placid sloshing back and forth of the blood, as many Galenists held. His very title, *De motu cordis*, called attention to the "*motion*" of the heart and blood. For him, the emphasis is not on the homeostatic balance of humors or on the circular design of the system as such, but on the activity of the blood, on its urgent and forceful impulsion. The sense of blood in motion was surely congenial to the energetic investigator, whom Arundel describes in a letter as "the little perpetual mov[ement] called Dr Hervye" (qtd. Keynes 31). Thus the excitement of the discovery itself, announced in Harvey's Baconian rhetoric, matches the breakthrough of finding it: a "new pathway for the blood must therefore be prepared and thrown open." What has been "thrown open" (as if actively brought to view rather than passively uncovered) is the body's inmost secret life: not its contemplative soul but the hard evidence of a throbbing, *vita activa* in the coursing circular flow of the blood. In a newly implied correspondence, the energy and generative power of the scientific enterprise find their sympathetic response in very phenomena disclosed by the inquiry.

Given the persistent, if not inevitable, analogy in the age of Arundel between the body and the body politic, the debate about the significance of Harvey's work in its own cultural context has centered as much on its "unmistakable political resonances" (Rogers 21) as on its scientific content. Christopher Hill saw in Harvey's later treatise *De circulationis sanguinis* (1649) a shift from the implicitly 'royalist' politics of the earlier *De motu cordis* to an implicitly 'republican' politics (perhaps opportunistically) attuned to the moment; for in the earlier work, Harvey had declared the heart the monarch of the body centrally responsible for imparting vitality and motion to the blood and, in turn, to the outlying organs, while in the later work he appeared to adopt an opposing view in which the blood contained its own impulsive and vitalist power. Others can imagine Dr. Harvey's horror at the thought that some covert anti-monarchical sympathies might be detected in his theories (e.g., Whitteridge). Nonetheless, among these critics, John Rogers argues that in its view of the blood as capable of autonomous action, Harvey's work of 1649 reflects an anti-authoritarian "vitalist moment" in which (anticipating Milton's monism) matter is conceived as infused with the power of reason and motion, and hence no longer in need of central control (2). In the context of such body-political readings, I should rather emphasize the immediate resonances of Harvey's circulatory model for the maritime ventures of his patron.

The heroic blazing of the "new pathway for the blood" not only sets the tone for other medical "conquests" inspired by Harvey's pioneering work in the years following the publication of *De motu cordis*. Inevitably, it also set in motion a sympathetic connection between Harvey as an explorer of the *mare internum* and those other famous "circulators" who opened new sea passages to navigation and trade. Thus, in verses prefixed the 1653 translation of Harvey's later study *De generatione animalium*, the noted physician and sometime poet Martin Llewellyn praised Harvey's achievement in the *De motu*, for which he was now justly famous:

> There didst thou trace the *Blood*, and first behold
> What *Dreames* mistaken Sages coin'd of *old*.
> For till thy *Pegasus* the *fountain brake*,
> The *crimson Blood*, was but a *crimson Lake*.
> Which first from Thee did *Tyde* and *Motion* gaine,
> And *Veins* became its *Channel*, not its *Chaine*.
> With *Drake* and *Ca[ve]ndish* hence thy *Bays* is curld,
> Fam'd *Circulator* of the *Lesser World*. (xv)

In the "lesser world" of man, Harvey has remapped the global voyages of the great circumnavigators and so joined their heroic company. He has broken the chains (both of old, mistaken ideas and the chains stretched across the mouths of rivers to keep ships out) and opened the channels for the "crimson" blood's triumphant and unimpeded navigation of the body. Llewellyn's imagery recalls those most stirring passages in Harvey's *De motu* in which the "blood" is half personified in a mini-narrative of circulation as a voyage to the "extreme and outward parts" of the world and back:

> For we see motion generating and keeping up heat and spirits under all circumstances, and rest allowing them to escape and be dissipated. The blood, therefore, becoming thick or congealed by the cold of the extreme and outward parts, and robbed of its spirits, just as it is in the dead, it was imperative that from its fount and origin, it should again receive heat and spirits, and all else requisite to its preservation—that, by returning, it should be renovated and restored. (74)

Here Robert A. Erickson sees the outline of a "long circuitous mission" on which the blood is dispatched, finally returning to the heart "where it is restored for its next journey" (81). This narative in turn carries the trace of "the ancient idea that the life-giving masculine life force is depleted by the insatiable female body" (81). As well, I would add, it carries the trace of a romance quest in which the hero barely avoids being killed in some inhospitable and monstrous realm of "the dead" before returning to the court from which he began. Even more specifically, Harvey imagines circulation as a voyage of discovery. Far from their home port in the heart and kept up in spirit by the initial motion of the vessel, the sanguine sailors are prone to dissipation if allowed too much rest. At the extremes of the journey, at the outer edges of the world, lies the threat of death from the cold if the ship is trapped in the ice or, as befalls travelers, of being "robbed" in uncordial places. If, as was common, the new world was imagined as a woman, they ran the further danger besetting mariners since the time of Odysseus and Aeneas, of having their manly energies sapped by female wiles.

But even here in the realm of the dead, whence sailors bring tales of anthropophagi and men whose heads do grow beneath their shoulders, lies the heartwarming prospect of the voyage home. Every circuit of the blood enacts a drama of near-death and ultimate *renovatio* in a return to the *fons et origo* of one's being. As Harvey's Latin makes clearer than the English translation, these terms resonant both of the fount of religious truth and the origins of art and empire in Greece and Rome are imported into the discourse of the body. Here they not only "trace" the larger circuits of English voyaging, whether for the planting of colonies like the one Arundel would hope to establish on Madagascar in 1638 or for the collection of antiquities; they also imbue it with a special vigor. If the exploits of "fam'd Circulator[s]" such as Drake and Cavendish inform a narrative of the circulation of the blood, then in turn the circulation of the blood grounds actual voyages to the extremities of the world in the natural processes of bodily life. What returns in the flow from the regions of the "dead"—classical marbles, inscriptions, coins—is also thereby warmed and renewed by the sun of Arundel's patronage, the vigorous movement of the cultural circulatory system itself a sign of throbbing good health.

Harvey and Arundel first met when their interests converged in the body of one Thomas Parr, a Shropshireman who died in November, 1635 at the reputed age of 152 years and nine months (Keele 37–38; Keynes 30–31). In Harvey's own account of the matter, "This poor man having been visited by the illustrious Earl of Arundel when he chanced to have business in those parts (his lordship being moved to the visit by the fame of a thing so incredible) was brought by him from the country to London: and having been most kindly treated by the earl both on the journey and during a residence in his own house, was presented as a remarkable sight to his Majesty the King" (*Works* 587–88). When Parr proceeded to die, however, Harvey—as then Physician in Ordinary to the King—was requested by Charles himself to perform an autopsy. The results confirmed that Parr's circulation was unobstructed and his organs free of disease. In such a remarkable state of preservation, the ancient might have still lived on if he had not been exposed to the fetid air of London and the unaccustomed luxury of a "table loaded with a variety of viands" and "strong drink" (*Works* 592). Brought from the outward parts of the land to the fount and origin of civility at Arundel House, Parr, it might be said, was robbed of his spirit (the official cause of death was listed as suffocation). His new patron must have seen Parr as a living antiquity to be collected and put on display—with the attendant irony that the same careful attempts at conservation that restored the Earl's antique statues and inscriptions in this case promptly killed off the main exhibit.

Harvey was never a resident at Arundel House like such other living members of the Earl's collections as Junius, John Selden, cataloguer of the Arundel Marbles, and the clergyman- mathematician William Oughtred who, plucked like the less fortunate Parr out of his obscure country parish, was given a room and induced by the Earl to write the *Clavis mathematicae,* the *Key to Mathematics,* on which his subsequent reputation would rest. Harvey preferred the hospitality of the King at Hampton Court, for there he was provided with a steady supply of royal deer for his experiments on the generation of animals. Still the Earl was particularly drawn to "Little Dr Harvey" both by personal affection and by an intellectual sympathy for the man who had found the key to unlock the pathways of the heart.

At the Earl's invitation Harvey accompanied Arundel as his personal physician on an embassy to Vienna in 1636. With Arundel bogged down in negotiations with the Emperor Ferdinand, Harvey used the several months of fruitless delay to go an extended side trip that took him as far south as Rome. Although his chief interest lay in visiting a series of medical colleagues, one letter surviving from that embassy refers to "honest little Harvey whom the Earl is sending to Italy about some pictures for his Majesty" (Keele 39). Harvey having rejoined the mission at its conclusion, Arundel's party returned to England. They paused in

Nuremberg to acquire the major part of the Earl's collections of drawings and manuscripts, many from the cabinet of the renowned Wilibald Pirkheimer, patron of Dürer and Erasmus.

I began by referring to Harvey's place in the history of medicine as the author of the *De motu cordis*. I hope to have shown how, at its origin, his work on circulation had an imaginative resonance in the Arundelian culture of the 1630s beyond its ultimate contribution to science. Harvey's other, less well known but equally passionate research interest is suggested by the autopsy report on Thomas Parr, who turns out to have been a remarkably vigorous piece of antiquity. In one passage, the physician notes for the record (and not without a hint of wonder) that despite his great age, Parr's "organs of generation were healthy" and his testes "sound and large." By common report, as Harvey also notes, Parr "did public penance for incontinence, after he had passed his hundredth year" (*Works* 589). What the history of medicine has relegated to a footnote is that during the same period, even as he continued his researches on the circulatory system, Harvey was assiduously performing experiments and compiling his observations on the sex lives of chickens and of the King's deer. These materials would ultimately be published in 1651 as the *De generatione animalium*, a treatise far longer than *De motu cordis*.

For Harvey, the study of the heart led back, inevitably, to the question of generation. As he observes at the beginning of the *De generatione*, the heart is the "first particle of the future foetus…formed from the menstrual blood in the uterus" immediately after the sexual act. As if preserving the sexual energy of its formation, the mature heart, in Harvey's account is "erected," and "being grasp'ed in ones hand whilst it is in motion, feels harder" (*De Motu* 19–20). At the other end of life, the heart is the last organ to fail and can, indeed, often be coaxed temporarily "back to life" even after its beating has ceased. Comparing the insistent beating of the heart even past the moment of death to the "leaping" of the sperm in coitus, Harvey sees "Nature in death making as it were a recapitulation, return[ing] upon her self with a retrograde motion, from the end of her race to the beginning of it, from whence she first issues thither she returns" (*De Motu* 32). Erickson cites these passages as evidence of a "phallic heart" also to be found in the early English novel (ch. 2). For our purposes, it is important to emphasize instead that the journey of life itself becomes a circulatory process—the heart recapitulating its own history, recalling in its final, insistent pulsations, its origins in the muscular contractions at the moment of procreation.

Thus an understanding of the heart might well unlock the key to an understanding of conception itself. Yet Harvey's work in embryology is nearly forgotten because it was not marked by any dramatic breakthrough that would count in the historical record as a "discovery." Indeed, for all his meticulous description of developing chicken eggs and deer fetuses and of the reproductive habits of their parents, an experimental solution to the basic problem of conception eluded him. None of the observable consequences of coition—including the primal formation of the heart—could explain its unseen and unfathomable origin. Where the study of the heart had led forward to the triumphant opening of a new "pathway" between the arteries and the veins, for Harvey and his successors in this field many years afterward, the study of reproduction could only lead back to an unanswerable question. Between the male and the female, what pathway led to the creation of a new life? No certain explanation presented itself, but Harvey's attempts to find one reveal an unexpected sympathetic link between art and biology within the Arundel circle.

The difficulty of discovering the *fons et origo* of life was compounded for Harvey by his mistaken but unwavering belief that "there is nothing which can be perceived by the senses in the uterus after coitus" (448). Undoubtedly, the "virtue proceeding from the male in coitus has such fructifying power that it changes the whole female both in her attitude of mind and in her bodily vigour" (444). Yet the mystery of how this fructifying power produces its effect only deepens, for as Harvey believes, "the male sperm either falls out again in a short while or vanishes away, and the blood [of the female, the fluid she contributes to coitus], having made its circuit, goes back again from the uterus through the vessels" (444). How can the female conceive when the flow of blood has passed through the uterus only to complete its voyage carrying no evident cargo of male sperm? The problem is articulated for the first time in the treatise, and most plaintively, during Harvey's discussion of the apparent fertilization of the chicken egg by "the mere touch of coition accomplished in a moment": "What is this thing thus handed on, that cannot be found either remaining, or touching, or perceptibly contained, yet performs its office with consummate wisdom and foresight, beyond all the bounds of art, and which even when it has departed and vanished makes the egg fertile, not because it now touches it but because it once touched it…as if the Almighty should say 'Let there be offspring,' and straightway it is so?" (189).

The same question (which, in another context, might be posed of an Apelles or a Zeuxis, the fertilizing influence of whose "consummate wisdom" remains, but whose once visible works have "departed and vanished") returns at the end of the treatise in a final chapter devoted to conception in humans:

> But because it is certain that the male's sperm does not penetrate into the hollow of the uterus, still less abide there for any time, therefore that sperm confers fecundity by some kind of contagion only, not as being something now touching and operating, but as something which once touched in the past. It does indeed seem that a woman, after spermatic contact in coitus, is made fecund by no perceptible corporeal agent, and is affected in the same way in which iron touched by a magnet is immediately endowed with the virtue of the lodestone and draws other iron bodies to itself. (443)

In this formulation, as Pagel observes, conception does not occur by any direct or continuous action of matter upon matter, but "by virtue of *sympathy*," an action "prompted by a mere touch that has taken place in the past" (251).

Under such assumptions, conception becomes an instance, the primordial instance, of sympathetic action at a distance. The semen has a profound and protracted effect on the uterus, an effect that not only follows upon the momentary act of coition, but exerts its power long after any corporeal evidence of its presence in the woman's body has disappeared. If, indeed, conception is achieved sympathetically in the first place, it can hardly be a coincidence that so many of Digby's examples of the workings of sympathy have to do with childbirth—as if a baby born with facial spots resembling the beauty marks his fashionable mother had affected during pregnancy were only completing the sympathetic process begun at his conception. The problem resolves itself into the very same problem faced by Digby in explaining how the Powder of Sympathy can cure Howell's injured hand, not as something touching the hand directly but only by coming into contact with the bandage that touched it in the past.

In the absence of any "perceptible corporeal agent," Harvey can only speculate, as he does in the passage cited above, over a range of possible causes for this sympathetic action, including magnetism and "contagion." The "virtue of the lodestone" had frequently been adduced to suggest that magnetic attraction lay behind such sympathetic cures as the weapons-salve, which had the power to draw an infection from the wound back to the blade that had caused it. William Gilbert himself, while skeptical about sympathetic cures, devotes several pages of the *De magnete* to the medicinal uses of the magnet (55–58). Robert Fludd, a defender both of sympathetic cures and Harvey's theory of circulation, argues in his *Philosophia moysaica* (1638) that in the little world of man, the blood may be compared to lodestone extracted from the "veins" of the earth (Debus 415). If so, then conception itself might be said to tap powers deep in the bowels of the earth to draw the male virtue to the female blood—in effect to "magnetize" the blood with that virtue—even though the semen and the uterus are not in direct "touch."

Similarly, Harvey regards "contagion" as another process capable of producing distant (and apparently incorporeal) effects. The daily wonder of generation may perhaps be understood as a kind of contagion by which beings and diseases alike "propagate," for "epidemic, contagious, and pestilential diseases scatter their seeds, or some other fomites, abroad through the air, and so propagate and produce in the bodies of other, diseases like to themselves, and so quietly multiply themselves in some hidden manner, through some kind of generation" (190). As any physician's experience with the plague would indicate, contagious diseases may somehow linger invisibly on walls or in bedclothes long after a patient's removal from the room, ready to contaminate the next victim. While "seeds" links this propagation of disease to the male virtue in animal procreation, Harvey's term "fomites" is more properly translated from the Latin *fomes* as "tinder." The dissemination of disease as a sudden sparking into life completes the circle from conception to death, as Harvey evokes the fiery power of epidemic disease to "bring widespread destruction to men and beasts" (190).

Harvey brings Digby to mind again as he goes on to consider other explanations:

> Some philosophers of our own time have refurbished the ancient opinion concerning atoms, and therefore believe this contagion, as also all other, to proceed from the most subtle effluvia coming from the semen of the male and emanating freely, after the manner of odours, to be shot into the uterus at the time of coitus. Others call incorporeal spirits on the scene, like so many demiurges, or angels or demons. Others understand a contagion as being like a ferment or a leavening. Others suppose other things and imagine differently. (448)

Among all this welter of opinion—not excluding Digby's atomism—Harvey has his own conjecture to offer, one that arguably could have germinated for him only through his sympathetic connection with Arundel as a patron of the arts and a collector of antiquities.

In the course of his dissections of the King's deer, Harvey is fascinated to observe that the uterus ripe for conception "appears thicker and more fleshy." At its inner surface where the fetus will actually grow, "it becomes more tender and corresponds in smoothness to the inner parts of the ventricles of the brain" (445). From this remarkable observation the conclusion inevitably proposes itself:

> [S]eeing that the substance of the uterus that has been made ready for the conception is so very like the constitution of the brain, why may we not justly surmise that the function of each of them is also alike, and that what imagination and appetite are to the brain, that same thing, or at least something analogous to it, is awakened in the uterus by coitus and from this proceeds the generation of the egg? For the functions of both are called conceptions and both are immaterial though they be the principles of all the actions of the body.... [Thus] the natural conception arises in the uterus of a woman, even as the animal conception is made in the brain. (445)

We have already seen this equation between mental and uterine "conception" loosely implied in Digby's obstetrical anecdotes about the working of sympathy: the mother's mental conception of John the Baptist prompted by the picture over her bed leads to the conception of a hairy child. For Digby the picture functions incidentally as the stimulus of the mental image, and secondarily (one must imagine subtle hairy atoms floating down from the brain to the womb) of fetal development. For Harvey, on the other hand, the imagination offers a model of "immaterial" conception: the "same thing" as occurs in the brain with the generation of thought, "or at least something analogous to it," is engendered by coitus in the brain-like concavities of the fertile uterus. Furthermore, for Harvey, artistic creation is intrinsic to both conceptions:

> And from this desire [of the female for the male] or conception it happens that a woman produces offspring like to the male progenitor. For just as we fashion from the conception of a form or an idea in the brain its likeness in the works of our hands, so does the idea or appearance of the genitor remaining in the uterus generate a foetus like to himself by the help of the formative faculty, that is to say, by imposing upon its own workmanship its own immaterial appearance. It happens in the same way as Art, which is the ειδοσ or form of the future work, produces its like when it is acting and begets it in the material. Thus the painter expresses a likeness through the intermediary of the conception and gives it actuality by imitating the conception that is internal to the brain, and builder also erects a house from his previously-had conception. (445–46)

For the first—and very likely, only—time in the history of embryology, a theory of painting forms the basis of a theory of conception, both sharing the conception of an immaterial Idea realizing itself in the material. The "idea" of the father remains in the uterus, sparked into life there by coition, after the semen has disappeared. Like an idea in the mind of the painter, this postcoital idea expresses its own likeness in the flesh of the mother's body, as on an intrauterine canvas prepared to receive it. The artist's *concetto* becomes the uterus's "conception." At the center of the mystery of life's origins, Arundel's physician finds the same creative process as his librarian had documented for the Earl as the origin of painting.

Thus, in *The Painting of the Ancients*, Junius cites Cicero's account of the fabled sculptor Phidias, who "when he made the images of Jupiter and Minerva, [did not] fixe his eyes upon one after whom he should draw such a similitude; but there did abide in his minde an exquisite forme of beautie, upon the which he staring, directed both his Art and his hand to the similitude of the same." In this "conceived figure," which Plato calls the "Idea," the artist finds a perfection and excellence beyond what can be seen, and this excellence he tries to embody in his handiwork (20). The theory not only describes an ancient formulation of artistic creativity recurrent especially in Neoplatonic and Mannerist theorizing in the Renaissance, it also rationalizes Junius's own scholarly project. For insofar as Junius could no more see the lost works of Phidias than Harvey could see anything in the womb after the semen had left the scene of conception, his account must itself be the realization of an immaterial idea of Phidias's perfection as an artist, just as that perfection lay originally in Phidias's idea of Jupiter and Minerva. In this sympathetic connection between Harvey and Junius, it may be said that ontology recapitulates art history. The biological development of the individual, and then of the generations of individuals in his family history, resolves itself into a kind of intellectual history, a history of ideas, insofar as the sequence of sexual procreations is mediated at every new generation by the immaterial agency of an Idea: conceptions and conceptions are the "same thing." Harvey himself further blurs the distinction between the two in the peroration to his chapter on conception, in which, at the end, he looks back at the history of scientific thought as a history of intellectual "begetting," and then imagines the future lineage of his own ideas—"for mind begets mind and one opinion another opinion":

> The atoms of Democritus and the chiefest good set in pleasure of Eudoxus fertilized Epicurus; the four elements of Empedocles, Aristotle; the doctrines of the ancient Thebans, Pythagoras and Plato; geometry, Euclid. After this same pattern a son is born like to his parents, and the virtues which ennoble a family and the hereditary vices are transferred sometimes after a long succession of years to the descendants.... Pliny says that among the people called the Dacians, every fourth generation the child born carries the marks of the family imprinted on its arm. The thoughts, opinions and customs which now hold the scene, why should they not return again many years hence after a time when these which are in use today have fallen into disuse? For the divine mind of the Eternal Creator which is imprinted in things begets its own image in human conceptions. (449–50)

One thinker "fertilizes" another, and like a familial birthmark reappearing in every fourth generation to "imprint" itself on the arm of the Dacian child, in the genealogy of the mind thoughts can return like recessive traits "many years hence." Thus Pliny's observation about the Dacians returns to fertilize Harvey's thinking about generation, just as in the passage above from Junius's *Painting of the Ancients*, the history of art turns into a history of the generation of a series of "conceived figures": the gods Jupiter and Minerva; the fabled sculptor Phidias, who had a perfect conception of them in his mind; Cicero, whose *De perfecto oratore* preserved the image of Phidias for future generations; and Junius himself, whose history revives all these images after many years, begetting his own conception in the mind of the reader.

As the painter supplies Harvey with a model of the immaterial Idea that imprints itself on the maternal womb, the physician in turn informs an Arundelian history of art in antiquity with a richly ambiguous image of "human conceptions." Seen from a point of view sympathetic to Harvey, that history can be conceived as engendering, and then filling, a gap between the ancient progenitors of art and Arundel, the patron whom Horace Walpole would call "the father of virtue" in England. Virtually all material evidence of those progenitors—among them, the astonishing works of such masters as Zeuxis, Parhassios, and Phidias—has disappeared. But the mystery at the very heart of procreation itself, as Harvey understood it, did not require the material trace of the father; indeed, it required his *absence.* Conception generates its power not as "something now touching and operating upon" future generations but as something which "once touched" us in the past, and has since utterly withdrawn. Individual texts, inscriptions, and works of art may reappear like the Dacian family birthmark many years hence. Ever dormant, but ever prepotent (not unlike the ancient William Parr), these ancient conceptions can be "awakened" again from their long historical sleep. Over the distance in time and space that separates us from antiquity, it is thus possible to establish a sympathetic connection. Like Digby's atoms sailing invisibly from a soaking bandage to a wounded hand, the surviving fragments of classical culture may act upon us to make us feel the influence of that distant world. We may be drawn to that world as by the attraction of a lodestone, but we may perhaps be able to reconceive it, vanished though it may be, as the first stirrings of a new life in the brain.

In this light we may look again at the Daniel Mytens portrait of Arundel seated before his sculpture gallery (fig. 1). The patron is separated from his collection of classical statuary by a portal which opens upon, and draws the eye into the depths of, a long gallery in which his acquisitions are ranged. The presence and visibility of these works of art only make more poignant a sense of our distance from them—indeed, of our being debarred entry to their space. It may be possible to retrieve the ruins of Apollo's temple at Delos, as Digby did, but can the spirit of the god be recalled from such a distance in time and space? The Earl sits before the door as both interlocutory figure and gatekeeper, his baton both directing our attention to his beloved statues and yet physically preventing our access. If, in fact, the long gallery did not yet exist as here pictured (see chapter 1), its being is to be located somewhere in the gap between the idea (in Arundel's mind) and the eventual reality (in Arundel's house). The painting, embodying the idea of the gallery in the illusion of a space created by tangible pigments on a material surface, combines the two. Insofar as it opens a conceptual space to be filled, in time, by the realization of Arundel's Ideal gallery, the Mytens looks forward to the concept of the Madagascar portrait, in which both the Earl's deeply contemplative expression and his possession of the objects at hand imply his ability to effect his colonial designs. The baton—the emblem of Arundel's potency, or his paternal ability to give life and (as Earl Marshall) to "create" titles—is an equally ambiguous conception. We know that it is confined to the space outside the gallery, but we also conceive it as penetrating that space as it reaches illusionistically backwards through the doorway and into the recess of the gallery. There it seems merely to touch the base of the statue of a woman second from the right in the row of sculptures. The touch of the patron's baton seems to spark the woman into life. At the distance of space and time but possessed of the Idea of antiquity, Arundel in his turn "confers fecundity" upon its material (and maternal) remains. Though as a type of the Venus *pudica* she covers herself modestly when she realizes she is being watched (by us?), her own gaze is magnetically attracted to the man she desires, who though he does not—cannot—look at her directly, has his own fertile conception of her in mind.

Conclusion: *The Tempest* as Prequel

For the purpose of a final reflection on Arundel, I would like to make two convenient, although not crucial, assumptions about the celebrations at court over the winter of 1612–1613, leading up to the wedding of the Princess Elizabeth and the Elector Palatine on St. Valentine's Day. One is that Arundel indeed attended the performance of *The Tempest* given as part of these extended nuptials—an assumption all the more likely in view of his prominence at court in these years, and especially of the visible role he played in the marriage festivities themselves (Hervey 70). The other assumption is that, unlike some of James's less sober courtiers and even the King himself, who was known to grow impatient with entertainments that seemed to interrupt the general roistering of the evening, Arundel was actually paying attention.

If he were, then he may have had occasion to meditate, thirty years later, on the Prosperan turn his own life had taken. After escorting the bridal pair across the Channel and back to the Palatinate, Arundel continued on to Italy, crossing over from Basle into Prospero's Milan. Thence, in the company of Inigo Jones, Selden, and the antiquarians Sir Robert Cotton and Sir William Dugdale, he spent more than a year exploring the art and architecture of the peninsula before returning to England in November, 1614. After this tour, the "Collector" Earl became increasingly absorbed in what would become his life's passion, his pictures and statues and the private studies surrounding them. Holding himself above the fray of court life, he was, as Prospero says of himself, "all dedicated / To closeness and the bettering of my mind" (1.2.8–0). Arundel left England for good in 1642, this time escorting Queen Henrietta Maria and the Princess Mary to safety in Holland—Arundel had the year before negotiated the marriage of the Princess to the young Prince of Orange, only to witness the collapse of her father's cause—before continuing on once more to Italy, where he died four years later.

One can imagine at least the possibility that Arundel was struck by the irony of a life that so exactly reversed the romance plot of Shakespeare's play. His first overseas commission of 1613 was to accompany the royal Ferdinand and Miranda of that long-gone wedding season to their new home. His last, following upon the wedding of another Princess was, in effect, to preside over a royal separation as he conducted her mother, Charles's queen, into exile. Arundel's own banishment from a world turned upside down by civil war was no less decisive than if he had been betrayed by some perfidious Antonio, but for him there would be no providential return. His letters from those last years indicate that his every third thought was the grave (Hervey 434).

Characteristically, in two ways we have seen in the chapters above, Arundel chose to cast himself in a role reminiscent of Prospero's. First, in the portraits of him by Mytens and Van Dyck, the ever-present staff of the Earl Marshall signifies a power that is at once judicial, disciplinary, and magical. In the Mytens portrait of Arundel seated before his sculpture gallery, its mere touch seems to "discover" the space in which the statues are ranged and, indeed, to bring them to life. Arundel's touch, like the touch of the artist's brush, can "create" these statues, his own art vying with the cold nature of the stone, just as in his role as the chief heraldic officer of the realm he can certify the creation of titled nobility. At once paternal and patronal, this life-giving gesture combines a theatrical revelation of the marvelous with the power to revive the ancient worlds represented by these marbles—to "transplant," as Peacham had said, old Greece and Rome into England.

Second, the Madagascar portrait and the project it represents transplant the fantasy of that creative power from the little world of the gallery to the larger world of a remote island colony, Arundel imagining (against all hard-headed likelihood) that, like Shakespeare's Gonzalo, he had "plantation of this isle" (2.1.141). Still in 1639, if not three years later, it seemed to him even in his ill health and darkening melancholy that he could escape misfortune by choosing a kind of voluntary exile which would hold the promise a new beginning amidst the fabled "riches and plenty" of Madagascar (Hervey 506). The Madagascar portrait also grounds Arundel's power in the books and antiquities that signify his preeminence as a collector. His success not only in recovering the artworks of the classical world but in providing for them, through such books as Junius's and Selden's, an historical as well as an architectural setting in Arundel House, establishes his authority as the sponsor of a colonial venture. The antiquities displayed in these paintings—both the ancient works preserved as objects in themselves, and those represented in the paintings commisioned by Arundel—figure as a kind of cultural capital dug up from ancient soil and now available for reinvestment in fresh enterprises. Thus Arundel has established his "Creditt wth the world," as he is led to hope in the public advertisement for the Madagascar scheme: both the confidence and the solvency to "disabuse such as shall thinke this is a vayne & ayrye undertaking" (Hervey 506).

The Earl's career as antiquarian and would-be colonialist sheds a retrospective light on Shakespeare's play as an allegory *avant la lettre* of English colonial expansion. Many recent attempts to read *The Tempest* as the harbinger of European attitudes toward the broadening vistas of overseas settlement and commercial exploitation place too much emphasis on Miranda's enthusiasm for a "brave new world," and not enough on the implications of Prospero's response to his daughter's famous exclamation: "'Tis new to thee" (5.1.18–4). The innocent Miranda has, at that moment, not only mistaken the bedraggled court party for a "new" race of creatures. Her father's reply reminds us that, in fact, there is nothing new in this world of the island—or rather, that what is perceived as new has been recollected here, as the shipwrecked and exiled remnant of the old. Prospero's remark thus touches upon one theme of the colonial narrative that will be most fully developed in Robinson Crusoe's laborious (re)construction of his own island domain out of the wreckage of the ship that carried him there.

To imagine the plantation of the new world as a material and cultural transplantation of the old is to realize how deeply *The Tempest* is invested in salvaging its own past from the "dark backward and abyss of time" (1.2.50). In the process of its completion, *The Tempest* reconnects Miranda's "brave new world" to old worlds faintly but profoundly invoked. Prospero's "Tis new to thee" opens a dual perspective in which the future is to be regarded as an aspect of its past—a past which must not only be remembered, as Miranda is prompted to recall the fleeting impressions of her childhood, but represented, as Prospero re-presents (and so foils in retrospect) his brother'streacherous plot.

Also to be retrieved from the same abyss of time is the series of events leading up to the time of the play itself: the banishment of Prospero's witchly alter ego, Sycorax, from her Africa homeland in "Argiers," the history of Caliban and Ariel, the virtual banishment of Alonso's daughter Claribel from Naples to her hateful marriage in Tunis. For a play supposed to embody the nascent spirit of a colonialist mentality, *The Tempest* is resolutely "backward" in the sense of its own place in time, far more powerful as a meditation on its own prehistory than in any glimpse it offers of a possible future. These proximate histories, moreover, evoke others even more remote. The name "Sycorax" is linked etymologically to that of the seductress Circe (see Kermode 26), who was also exiled to a Mediterranean island, where she long ago turned men into beasts. Algiers may have its own more deeply buried amorous history as the putative site of Carthage. It was from there that Aeneas fled the entangling coils of a women in order to pursue his destiny in Rome—thereby setting an ancient example of civic duty that may stand as a rebuke to Prospero's indifference to his public office while he was Duke of Milan. In the course of the banter between Sebastian and Antonio about the "widow Dido" (2.1.9–00), Antonio's ironic allusion to the "miraculous harp" of Amphion that raised the walls of Thebes (2.1.85) juxtaposes a resonant image of civilization-building with a reminder of its destruction, in this case the utter obliteration of Carthage that makes its very location a matter of dispute. Of the various nations peopling the "Africa" of the Renaissance imagination, Sycorax also has an unspecified but compelling association with the elusive nation of the Amazons.

Louis Montrose reminds us of Ralegh's speculation in the *Discovey...of Guiana* (1596) "on the existence of Amazons near the river named after that mythical but seemingly international tribe of 'warlike women': 'The memories of the like women are very ancient as well in Africa as in Asia.... In many histories they are verified to have bene, and in divers ages and provinces'; [Ralegh] then speaks of 'the Amazones' as if 'they' were at once the very ancient contemporaries of the Trojans and the actual women before his eyes: 'if they conceive, and be delivered of a sonne, they returne him to the father'" (26). The immediate plot of the play thus rests upon a partially-concealed historical deposit made up of pieces of other stories: of Aeneas and Dido, Amphion, Penthelesia the Homeric Amazon, Circe, and, as we may add among the tangled ancestry of Sycorax, the Ovidean Medea. These figures, though unseen, "people the isle," itself a blank play space located at an imaginative midpoint somewhere between Europe and Africa, the present and past.

This archaeological configuration of the colonial landscape returns us to the Arundelian arts of colonization. In the Van Dyck *Madagascar* portrait, showing the Earl as a latter-day Gonzalo imagining his ideal commonwealth, the antiquities also pictured there represent the pieces from his own collection that he is ready to bring into play as the cultural markers of a new island possession. The two heads in the portrait, the bronze "Arundel Homer" and the marble Apollo, suggest the connection of this project to the ancient poetry of epic achievement. They may recall for us the lines from Andrew Marvell's "Horatian Ode" (92) which glance back from the scene of the beheading of Charles I to that of a horrifying and ambiguous omen unearthed at the founding of Rome:

> So when they did design
> The *Capitol's* first Line,
> A bleeding Head where they begun
> Did fright the Architects to run.

No sooner is the "bleeding Head" discovered (Marvell is here following Pliny) than it is incorporated into a prophetic vision in which "the State / Foresaw its happy Fate." Nonetheless, Marvell's emphasis, and the thrust of his irony, is not on the prediction of future prosperity for Rome but on the emblem of repressed violence at its origin. All states, Marvell seems to imply at a moment of unprecedented political violence for the English nation, are for better or worse built upon bleeding heads; he also insinuates that it is in the interest of subsequent histories to conceal such capital crimes by reinterpretation, even though the originary violence they bespeak is preserved in the institutions of the state: the *Capitol* rests on the *caput*. Thus the "first line" does not mark the beginning of the enterprise but the dividing line between what the architects construct and its prior foundation. Like the line of sight connecting the antique heads to Arundel's in the portrait (as if the vision of Madagascar were no less his than the possession of Homer and Apollo), the political lineage drawn by Marvell leads the mind into the dark backward—doubling back from the origin of the Cromwellian commonwealth on the execution block in 1649 to rediscover the origin of Rome in a gruesome artifact. Arundel's own insubstantial "design" for a new world in Madagascar begins, and in his case ends, with an excavation of the old. I have argued that as the political and commercial manifestation, in England, of a Baconian faith in progress, a buccaneering exuberance, and the search for a new Jerusalem, the nascent expansionist *mentalité* of the Arundel years is, nonetheless, at least partially distorted when viewed through the lens of what "colonialism" and "imperialism" have come to mean for us. We tend to read modernity back into a culture motivated, we presume, by a desire to possess the future—in effect, to become us. The questions we ask from this point of view will obscure the fact that no one during Arundel's years had any clear idea of such a future, or of a consolidated empire outside the three kingdoms. In this, the vagueness of the Earl's fantasy about Madagascar is entirely typical. It would be more accurate to start with the assumption that Arundel's generation, for whom the word "original" had not yet taken on its modern meaning, tended to think of discovery also in its older sense as "uncovery" or rediscovery of the past. By this logic, exploration and antiquarianism occupy the same space. To demonstrate the imaginative force and subtlety of that logic in the work of the Arundel circle has been the purpose of this book.

Appendix: Davenant's "Madagascar"

One other monument to the idea of Madagascar survives, to be set next to Van Dyck's painting as both a representation of, and a spur to, a possible voyage of colonization. In 1638, the year of Junius's English edition of *The Painting of the Ancients*, and the year before Van Dyck's painting and Arundel's abortive venture, a vision of Madagascar also inspired William Davenant, just then reaching the height of his fame as a poet and dramatist. The son of an Oxford vintner, Davenant was reported by Aubrey to have boasted, when in his cups, that he was actually Shakespeare's bastard child. (Herschel Baker has observed that "Even if such gossip could be converted into fact, it would merely prove that Shakespeare's kind of genius was not transmitted by the genes" [252].) But with enterprise enough to make the most of his modest talents, Davenant followed in Ben Jonson's footsteps by collaborating with Inigo Jones on the production of two court masques, most notably *Britannia Triumphans* on the Sunday after Twelfth Night. His tragedy *The Unfortunate Lovers* played at the Blackfriars in April. At the end of 1638, in a personal triumph more richly symbolic than financially rewarding, he was granted a royal annuity of one hundred pounds to mark his appointment as Poet Laureate (Davenant xxv). In the course of this *annus mirabilis* in the career of the future author of *Gondibert*, Davenant published his first collection of verse, *Madagascar; With Other Poems* (London, 1638). As the title may imply—conflating as it does the name of the place with the name of the poem—in this inaugural volume poetic and colonial ambitions are launched on the same tide. Here the new poet will emerge, not, as Spenser did, by the publication of a Virgilian pastoral, but as the author of a brief epic of maritime conquest.

"Madagascar" is dedicated to Prince Rupert, the royal nephew already named after his arrival at the English court in 1636 as Viceroy of the distant island he would never see, much less conquer. As I have noted above, any initial excitement stirred by this commission seems to have faded in a few months. To have pursued the project would have meant facing the derision of those who thought the whole scheme a fool's errand, as well as the opposition of many members of the East India Company. Expanding its commerce in India in the same year as Arundel's Madagascar venture, East Indiamen would naturally be suspicious of "a plan which seemed likely to threaten their own trade interests in the area," if by some slim chance it should succeed (Davenant 343). Under the circumstances, the Prince was convinced of the greater urgency of returning to his military duties in the Palatinate, fighting for the Protestant cause.

Untouched by any such qualms, however, the poem reports Davenant's dream vision of Rupert's voyage to Madagascar in the company of two of the poet's most generous patrons, Endymion Porter and Henry Jermyn, men of substance whose names had briefly been associated with the venture.Once the party has landed on Madagascar, Davenant's unfolding reverie celebrates the defeat of a band of unspecified (but likely Portuguese) marauders through the valor of these two champions and their heroic commander, the Prince. With the victory secured, the victors are accorded their spoils. The wealth of the island, "the cause, and the reward of War" is "greedily explor'd" (Davenant, ll. 365–66).Rupert's triumph secures a strategically important island, "seated for predominance" astride the main trade route between east and west. To the poet's imagination, it is also an isle brimming with gold, pearls, precious stones, and even the "Black Suds of *Ambar-Greece*" (l.392) which, so claimed Boothby's account, were among the "rich commodities" of Madagascar (Davenant 350). Unlike Van Dyck's portrait of Arundel, Davenant's poem has proved to be of little enduring interest except as a contribution to the short-lived Caroline fantasy of a golden world in the Indian Ocean. At its moment, however, and seen in the broader context that subsumes both works, it reveals the network of cultural forces that gave the fantasy much of its political and imaginative power.

All of Davenant's work for the year 1638 is of a piece. Graham Parry among others has seen *Britannia Trimphans* as a defense of Charles's controversial ship money tax, and more generally of England's maritime expansion in the face of rampant brigandage and the commercial challenge posed by the growing naval power of the Dutch and the Portuguese (Parry 19–9; Howarth, "Politics" 8–6). In Davenant's masque the King himself appears before Inigo Jones's nautical backdrops as "Britanocles," who has swept the sea of pirates and brought on a reign of peace and prosperity for the arts and sciences. Thus the masque anticipates the theme and even the language of "Madagascar" as its first song ("Breake forth thou Treasure of our sight") praises the King's power on the seas:

> What to thy Power is hard or strange?
> Since not alone confinde unto the land;
> Thy Scepter to a trident change,
> And strait unruly Seas thou canst command!
> (Davenant 222, ll. –2)

In "Madagascar," nephew Rupert *triumphans* can also "command" wind and wave by means of his "mighty Uncle's Trident" (Davenant 11, l. 38), and once he reaches the island he can be assured of victory by the same emblem of royal power:

> For well our northerne Monarch knowes, howere
> The Sea is duly held, the proper spheare
> Wherein that Trident swayes, yet, in his hand
> It turns strait to a Scepter when on land[.]
> (Davenant 11, ll. 4–4)

In their boldest terms a (prescient) call for the use of sea power to extend Britain's dominion to foreign lands, these lines carry a subtler and reinforcing mythic resonance. The easy Ovidian transformation of scepter "strait" to trident, and trident "strait" back to scepter marks a series of other metamorphoses: the mythological and magical impulses of the masque into the colonial epic of the latter poem; Charles I into Neptune; Prince Rupert into his mighty uncle; military into naval power—and the sea into the land, as each element turns its "proper spheare" into the other, both now encompassed within the larger, unconfined sphere of kingly property.

As politics and prestidigitation merge in these two texts, so do the role of the poet as the subject of royal power and royal power as the poet's subject. In *Britannia Triumphans* the King in his guise as Britanocles seems almost literally able to astonish those who behold him:

> Why move these Princes of his traine so slow
> As taking root, they would to Statues grow,
> But that their wonder of his vertue turnes them so!
>
> 'Tis fit you mix that wonder with delight,
> As you were warm'd to motion with his sight,
> So pay the expectation of this night.
>
> (Davenant 223, ll 4–9)

So moved by their wonder at the appearance of Britanocles that they can hardly move, the living princes seem about to take a pleasantly Ovidian turn, "taking root" as Daphne did when she was transformed into the laurel, or growing "to Statues," and so very nearly turned into works of art by the royal arts of kingship. To the Caroline court, with more than a residual belief in the power of the King's touch and the awe compelled by his Presence, such a moment would have been regarded, if not as literal fact, then at least as something more than poetical fancy. But the specific theatrical resonance of "wonder," "motion," and "turn" (as in Inigo Jones's *machina versatilis*, the "turning machine" by which the King may well have been made to "appear") implies that such powers are in turn conferred upon the King by the authority of the masque. So, too, in "Madagascar," the entire expedition is produced by, and contained within, the poet's dream, however much it hopes to anticipate the fact. In the masque the figure mediating between the poet and the King is "Fame," who sings the lines quoted above. Fame personifies the repute which is the King's, finds its source in the King and its matter in his deeds, but also trumpets the poet's word and cannot find its inspiration except in his breath.

Fame thus turns us back to the poet. It is his fame that takes root in, and grows out of, the masque. It is he whose statue will stand as the endless monument of his fame even when the brilliance of the night's performance will have faded away. One mark of the poet's triumph is his command of both Donne and Jonson, immediate predecessors whose achievements Davenant is able to turn to his advantage. Davenant's "unruly Seas" rewrites the "unruly sun" of Donne's "The Sun Rising" and makes the same witty point. The "unruly" will now be brought under rule, regulated by a greater power—albeit now, the King's rather than the lover's. Here and elsewhere in the songs of this masque, Davenant's language echoes that of the *Songs and Sonnets*: "sight," "rise," "Hemisphere," "strait," "absence," but with the difference that poet who had restricted his explorations to the bedroom gives place to the one who taps the authority of the monarch of wit in the service of a prince for whom the better hemisphere lies off the coast of Africa, and not in the eye of the beloved. But when Fame begins by praising Charles, in the famous phrase of the Cary-Morison Ode, as the "faire example" by which "Heroique vertue findes her way" Davenant 222), it is the example of Jonson that the poet has before him.

The text of *Britannia Triumphans* was not published until 1673, but fortunately for Davenant's laureate ambitions, the *Madagascar* volume was, in 1638, in an edition prefaced by a medley of commendatory verses all testifying, in effect, that its own fame had preceded it. Like Jonson's self-consciously crafted folio of 1616, *Madagascar* not only collects Davenant's poems but authorizes them, offering the book itself as evidence of the poet's fame, the fair example of Davenant's literary virtue. As Prince Rupert is to Charles, the unspoken analogy of these allusions to Jonson suggests, so Davenant is to his great predecessor. The connection between literary and political authority is implied in the ambiguity at play in Jonson's, and then Davenant's use of the phrase, "faire example," joining the force of exemplary deeds with that of the legible hand of the recording poet.

Two of the commendatory poems are contributed by Sir John Suckling, the Son of Ben who would later include the reputedly syphilitic Davenant in "A Session of the Poets" as the only "laureate without a nose" (l. 48). Suckling's first poem at the head of the *Madagascar* volume echoes Carew's elegy on the death of Donne five years earlier ("Thou hast redeem'd us, *Will*") and then goes on to make the comparison explicit. Since Donne, the "great Lord" of wit "parted hence, no Man has ever writ / So neere him, in's owne way" (Davenant 7). In the second, Suckling marvels: "What mighty Princes Poets are!" Having no need to trouble themselves with money, victuals, or favorable winds for their imaginary voyages, poets "Discover, conquer, what, and where they please" (Davenant 7). Suckling's conflation of princes and poets identifies Davenant with his hero, although unlike Rupert, whose conquest of Madagascar was to be nothing more than a poetic fantasy, it was the poet who returned from his literary expedition with a substantial prize: "And now the newes in town is; *Dav'nant's* come / From *Madagascar*, Fraught with Laurell home" (Davenant 7).

In another commendation, William Habington adds that "Ev'n *Madagascar*…doth lie / A trophie now of thy Wits Victorie," sustaining the flicker of a Jonsonian ambiguity as to whether the name "Madagascar," like the name "Penshurst," refers to a poem or a place. Nor yet does the island disdain "destruction to her state, / Encompast with thy Laurell in her fate" (Davenant 9). Carew himself contributes a delicately bantering poem, noting that in the field of epic achievement, Davenant may well surpass even Homer and Virgil, the latter because, under Davenant's "warrant," Prince Rupert managed to avoid the amorous distraction that delayed Aeneas, "Conducting to remotest shores our force / (Without a *Dido* to retard his course)" (Davenant 7). All of this is summed up in retrospect in *The Great Assises Holden in Parnassus By Apollo And His Assessours* (1645), in which an anonymous critic cannot resist delivering his verdict on Davenant with another sidelong glance at the effect of the poet's syphilis on his appearance, "that all the world might know,"

> His art was high, although his nose was low:
> But *Madagascar* chiefly did express
> His raptures brave, and laur'ate worthiness.
> (Davenant lvi)

These conjunctions, observed by Davenant's first readers, between the colonial ambitions of the poem and the laureate and patronage ambitions of the poet are too frequent and too insistent to be coincidental. Both the expedition to Madagascar and the "laureate worthiness" earned in its recounting are epic achievements, each one dependent upon and a version of the other. In 1638, at this early moment in the history of British colonial acquisition, any thought of the conquest of Madagascar—whether Rupert's or Arundel's—was a mere flight of fancy, an airy nothing. Nonetheless it opens, in prospect, a blank space for the imagination to subdue and populate, creating a local habitation and giving it a name commensurate with its "worthiness." Davenant's choice of characters to populate this fancy underscores the nexus of patronage and colonization. For along with that of Prince Rupert, then a transient in the English court after all, the poem, as I noted above, also cultivates the regard of Davenant's most influential patrons, Endymion Porter and Henry Jermyn.

These two are given pride of place among the Prince's imaginary crew, the "two Brave *Heroes*," also praised in Carew's commendatory poem, "whom wee justly may / By *Homer's Ajax* or *Achilles* lay" (Davenant 8). Davanant was particularly indebted to Porter for having recommended him into the service of the Queen in 1635. To leave no doubt of his obligation, in the same volume Davenant addresses no less than seven other poems to the influential courtier, an honor befitting Charles's confidante, trusted diplomat, and agent in the purchase of paintings for the Royal Collection. Endymion Porter in turn supplies the first prefatory poem, "compell'd," as he claims, by the poet's "commands to write / I'th Frontis-peece of this" (Davenant 5). Despite his professed inability to do the poem justice in his praise, Porter declares Davenant's poem itself a jewel "which comes / From *Madagascar*, scenting of rich gummes." He concludes that "such a Poem, in so sweet a stile, / As yet, was never landed on this Isle," and he hints that in this poetical branch of the eastern trade, Davenant has brought home a cargo to be purchased at a higher rate than mere praise: "And could I speake your prayses at each *Pore* / Twere little for the worke; it merits more."

When, in Davenant's poem, the two champions Porter and Jermyn step forward to fight, they do more than defend the Prince's party against the imagined military threat to the landing in Madagascar. They already enjoy a reputation at court as the protectors of poets and musicians, having striven "to grace / The silenc'd remnant of poor *Orpheus* race" (Davenant 14, ll 169–70). Implicitly their cultivation of the artistic "race," as the heirs of Orpheus, the founder as well as the singer of civil order, augurs well for their success with other races, such as the "remnant" of the ten lost often tribes said to populate such places as Madagascar. Such is their magnanimity, they also "protect those who with wealthier fate, / Old *Zeuxis* lucky *Pensill* imitate" (Davenant 14, ll 173–74). These beneficiaries of our heroic patrons are painters like Van Dyck, "lucky," as Davenant may well suggest, because they receive more lavish commissions and stipends than any of their literary competitors, including Davenant with his comparatively paltry laureate annuity of one hundred pounds.

Thus the imagined military rivalry for possession of the island returns us to a *paragone* of poetry and painting, perhaps not by happenstance at a moment when the most celebrated practitioner of each of these arts in England—Davenant and Van Dyck—sets sets his hand to the image of Madagascar. Just as, for Davenant, the riches of Madagascar become the object of competition among nations, so the benevolence of Endymion Porter's patronage inspires the rivalry of Davenant and Van Dyck. Davenant's encomia on Porter in the *Madagascar* volume follow upon, and given his jab at the competition armed with "*Zeuxis* lucky *Pensill*," seem to emulate Van Dyck's *Self-Portrait with Endymion Porter* earlier in the 1630s (Prado; repr. Brown, pl. 152). As Christopher Brown notes, this "beautiful oval-shaped canvas" is the only portrait in which Van Dyck paints himself in the company of another sitter, suggesting at once the special intimacy of their friendship while preserving a sense of the difference between patron and client: "Van Dyck glances, a little tensely, over his shoulder, while Porter, by contrast, exudes relaxed *bonhomie*" (152).

What Porter has bestowed upon such favorites as Davenant and Van Dyck, he first receives himself as the chief beneficiary of the King's largesse. Rising from relatively modest origins, Porter was remarkable for the wealth and political power he amassed during the 1620s and 1630s while holding no formal office except as Groom of the Bedchamber to Charles I. Literally and figuratively at the very center of the patronage system, however, in this crucial place at court Porter became the conduit of influence to and from the King, and the guardian of access to the royal person. Curiously for one so strongly identified with the inner circle at Whitehall, Porter also fills another place, at least in the Caroline poetic imagination, as a fair example of "The Country Life." In this poem, Robert Herrick relocates Porter to the same moral landscape occupied by Jonson's Robert Sidney in "To Penshurst." Unenvious of his neighbors, attentive to the frugal management of his estate and satisfied with the simple pleasures of the shearing feast and the wassail bowl, Porter confines his ambition within its modest bounds, for "'tis not the extent / Of land makes life, but sweet content" (ll. 17–18).

It is a sign of the interdependence of "court" and "country" that Porter should come to symbolize both, and a sign of the tensions within this commonplace that the enjoyment of the "country life" should be conventionally portrayed in Herrick not as a respite from the hurley-burley of life at court, but as essentially opposed to it:

> Sweet country life, to such unknown
> Whose lives are others', not their own!
> But serving courts and cities, be
> Less happy less enjoying thee. (ll. 1–4)

The advantage of the country is that there, removed from the center where one's life belongs to others, one comes into one's "own," taking possession of the self. Less conventionally for such poems, in Herrick this rural self-possession is also bounded on the far side, geographically, by the same limited ambition that sets it off from the court. Just as Porter, in his "own dear bounds," draws the line at losing himself in the service of the court, so he restricts himself from any thought of expanding eastward into the spice trade or westward in search of gold:

> Thou never plow'st the ocean's foam
> To seek and bring rough pepper home;
> Nor to the Eastern Ind dost rove
> To bring from thence the scorched clove;
> Nor, with the loss of thy loved rest,
> Bring'st home the ingot from the West. (Ll. 5–10)

Herrick's country idyll locates Porter securely between two places not his own, the little world of the Bedchamber in which he can only serve others, and the big world of expanding opportunity, where he can only serve ambition.

It is this model of a delimited self, one responding both to a Jonsonian ethos of self-possession and to a Donnean agoraphobia, that Davenant revises by making his Porter the hero of a fantasy of exploration: what is to be one's own is found at the end of a voyage beyond the bounds, in the possession of an exotic island. Herrick's Porter is one of those happy men who have found "lives" of "their own" in a poetic effacement of the place where they actually lived, including the system of patronage which, though unspoken and denied in a vision of complete self–sufficiency, in fact underwrites this very poem dedicated in its title by Herrick to this most prominent patron. Davenant's Porter, in contrast, is constructed as a bridge between the two worlds Herrick excludes, the court and the Eastern Ind—reconfiguring at the same time the traditional geography of court power. Royal authority, as deployed through such agents as Rupert and Porter in Davenant's poem, is no longer conceived simply as emanating from the center and diminishing with distance from the source as a light fades into darkness (to invoke the central image of Orgel and Strong's "Platonic Politics"). This equation of authority with proximity to the King is literalized in the important "places" occupied by those privileged to be in the royal presence in the Bedchamber, the Privy Chamber, or even on the Stool. Authority may now be imagined alternatively as bipolar, deployed on a line between the King and the colonial possession claimed in the King's name. For Davenant, this is a distance spanned as much by the figure of Porter and the ties of patronage relations he represents as by the desire for cloves and peppers.

Among his diplomatic assignments, as a connoisseur and adviser on painters, Porter negotiated the details of shipping and installing the Rubens ceiling in the Banqueting House at Whitehall. For such services, Kevin Sharpe observes, he "was showered with grants and favours" by Charles: "royal lands, the customs on French wines, the farm of the wines at Chester, the surveyorship of the Petty Customs of the Post of London, the profits of the manufacture of white writing paper, and more" (Sharpe 164). The traffic in compliments between Davenant and Porter both in the text of "Madagascar" and in the pages of the surrounding volume suggests that, as a rich source of bounty, Porter is as much the immediate object of the poet's desire as the distant island is the goal of his poetical voyage. The two converge in the prospect just visible over the horizon of the poem, that if such an expedition were to succeed, such a man as Porter might well be further rewarded by the gift of colonial lands, the cultivation of which would increase his power to cultivate the race of Orpheus.

In the last of the commendatory poems in the *Madagascar* volume, William Habington comments on the broadening of Davenant's professional horizons as he moves beyond his successes as a dramatist to larger fields: "But here the Stage thy limit was. Kings may / Find proud ambition humbled at the sea / Which bounds dominion. But nobler flight / of poesie has a supremer right / To Empire, and extends her large command / Where ere th'invading Sea assaults the land" (Davenant 9).In this account of the "nobler flight" of poetic ambition, traditional images of the ascent of Parnassus have given place to an image of geographical expansion, and to a language of "dominion," invasion and assault, and the "right / To Empire." Such claims are startling, in the 1630s, in their anticipation of the rhetoric of two centuries of British colonial rule.We might conclude, in retrospect, that the language of colonial discourse has contaminated this description of a poetic *plus ultra*. It would be more accurate to think of it the other way around, to see that at this proto-colonial moment, the possibility of an unlimited dominion lies only in the hands of the poets. This is an empire of the imagination only, for which the conceit of a triumphant Britain "extending her large command" (Davenant 14, l. 181) becomes the perfect (extended) metaphor. The mention of Zeuxis (l.174) signals that the whole project of Madagascar shown here is a *trompe l'oeil*, like the fabled masterpieces of the Greek artist cataloged by Junius. Beneath the illusionistic surface of the image lie the more tangible concerns of artistic ambition and the rivalry for patronage expressed under the figure of the heroic voyage.

Illustrations

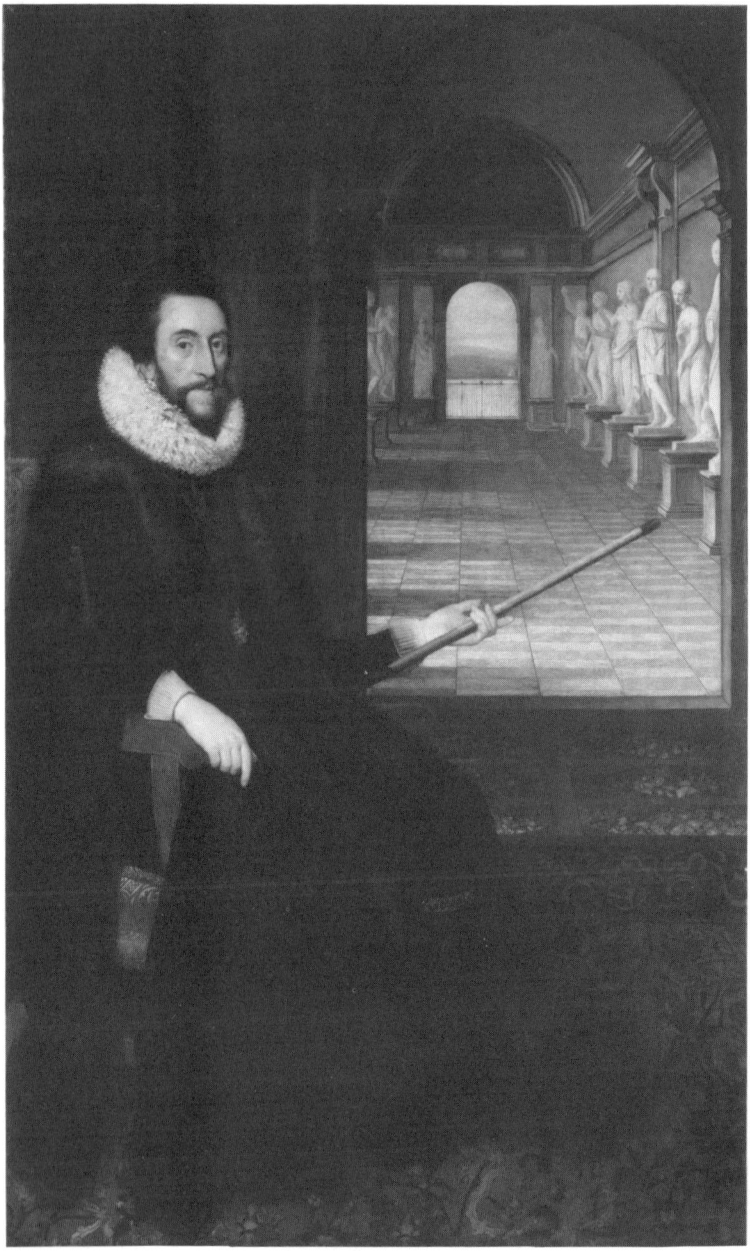

Figure 1. Daniel Mytens, *Thomas Howard, Earl of Arundel*, c.1616–1618

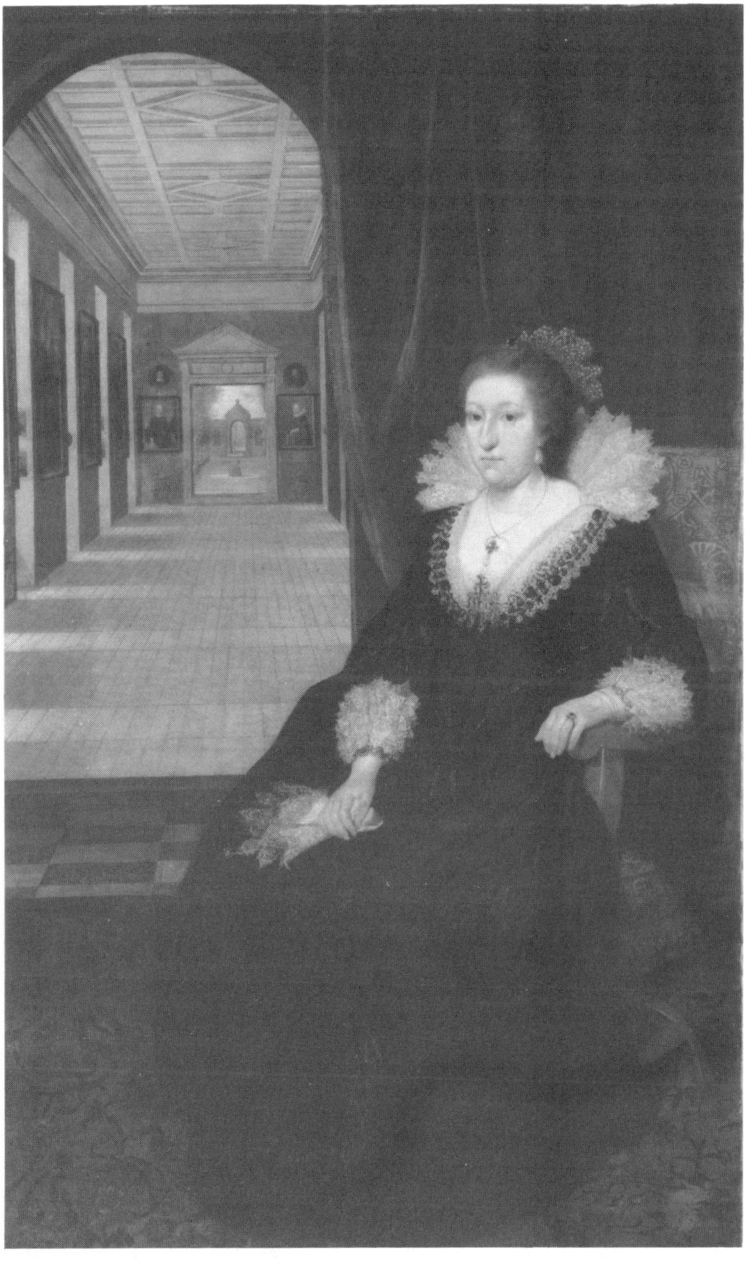

Figure 2. Daniel Mytens, *Aletheia, Countess of Arundel,* c. 1616–1618

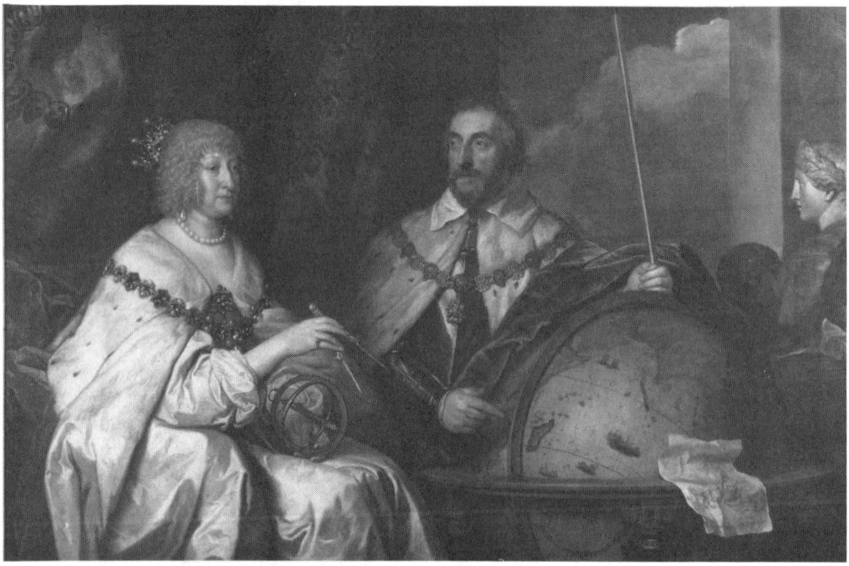

Figure 3. Anthony Van Dyck, *Thomas Howard, Earl of Arundel, and the Countess of Arundel* (The "Madagascar" Portrait), 1639

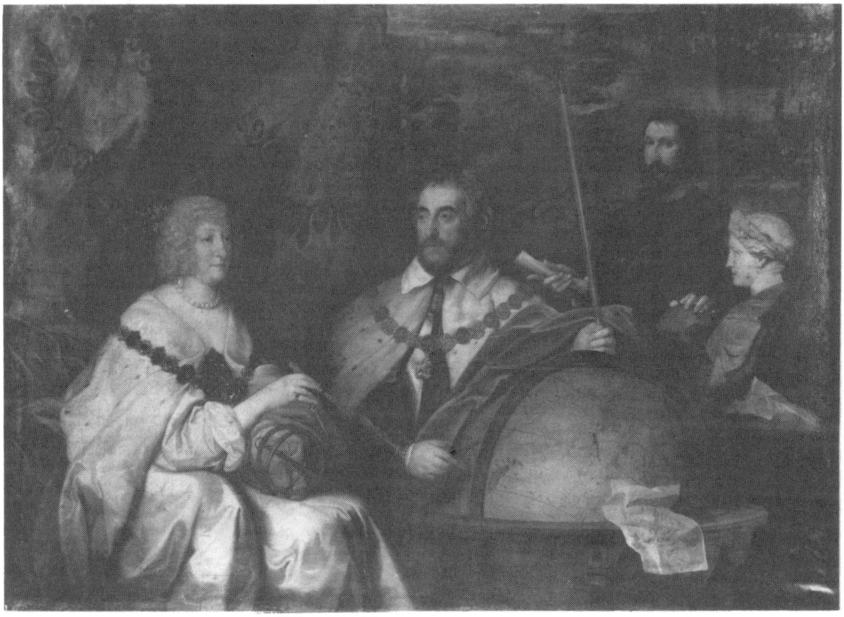

Figure 4. Anthony Van Dyck, *Thomas Howard, Earl of Arundel, and the Countess of Arundel* (The "Madagascar" Portrait), 1639, Knole version

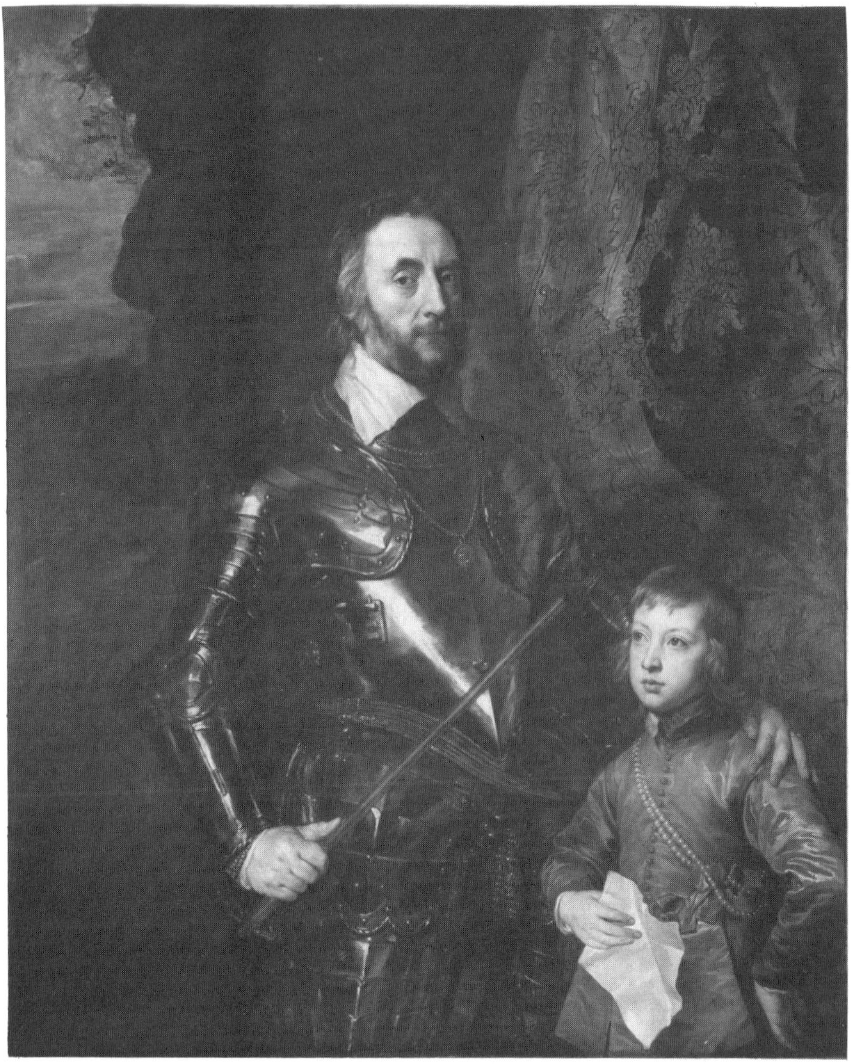

Figure 5. Anthony Van Dyck, *Thomas Howard, Earl of Arundel, and his Grandson, Lord Maltravers* c. 1635

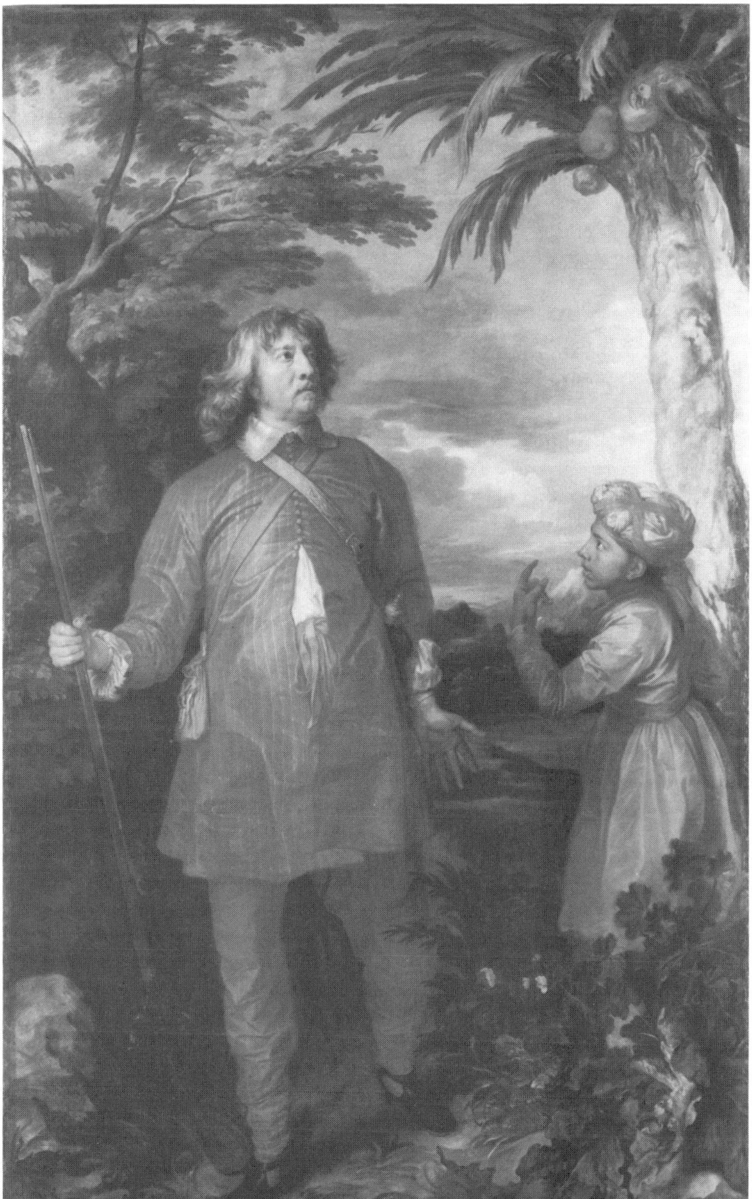

Figure 6. Anthony van Dyck, *William Fielding, Earl of Denbigh,* c.1633

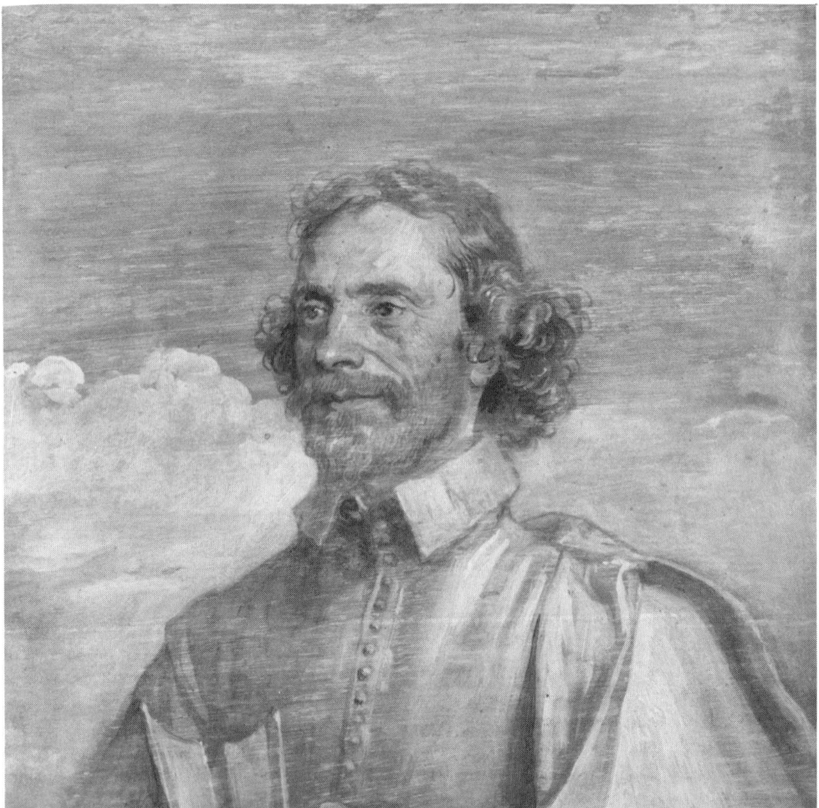

Figure 7. Anthony Van Dyck, *Franciscus Junius*, 1640

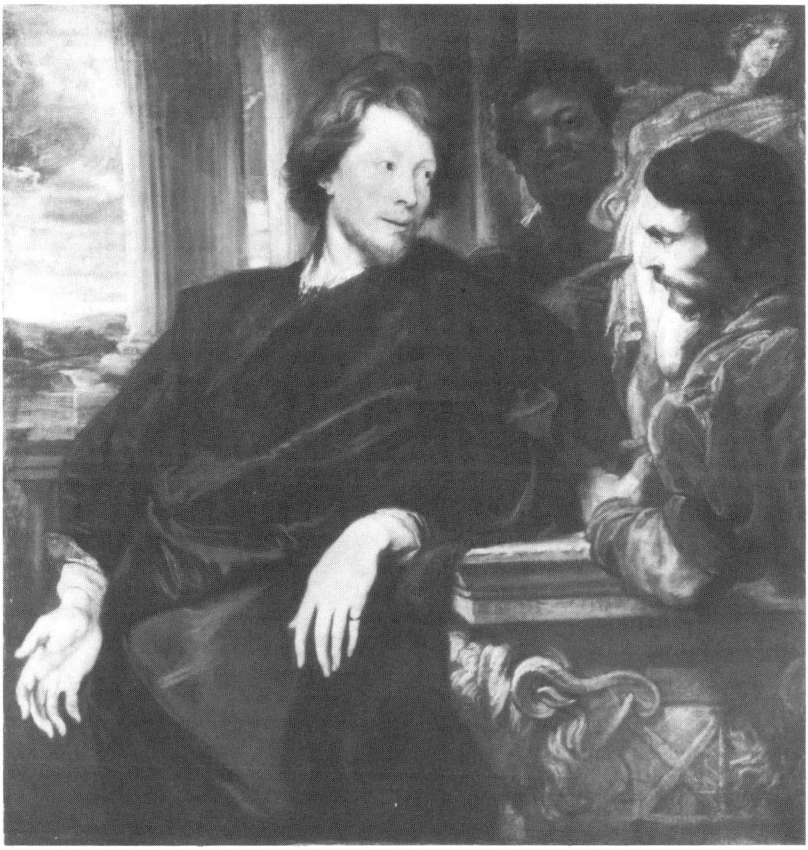

Figure 8. Anthony Van Dyck, *George Gage*, 1622–23

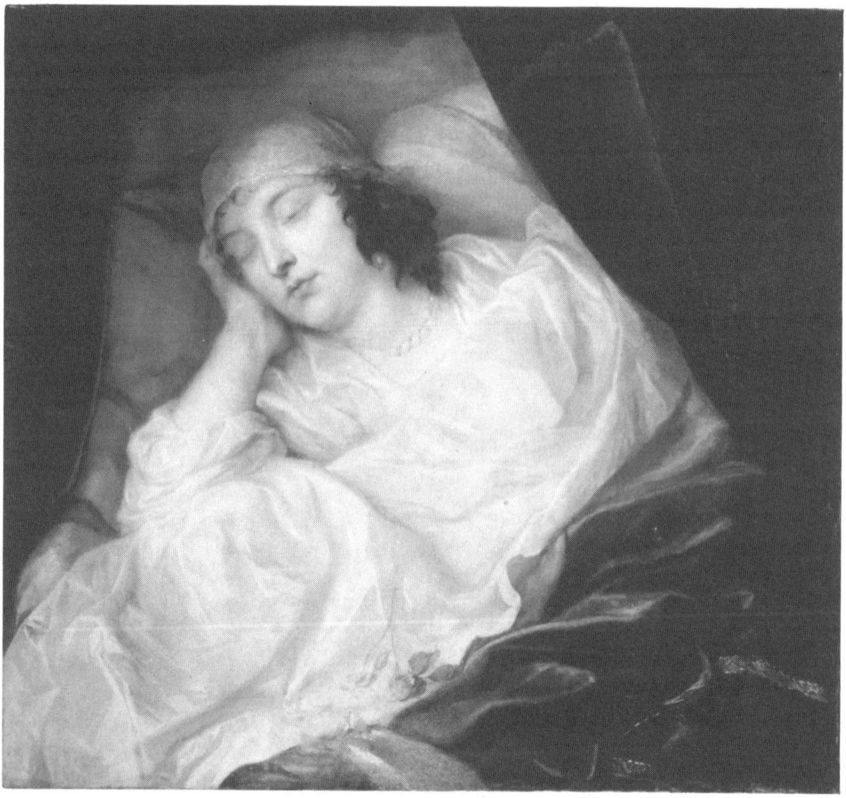

Figure 9. Anthony Van Dyck, *Venetia Stanley, Lady Digby, on her Deathbed,* 1633

Works Cited

Appleby, John C. "War, Politics, and Colonization, 1558–1625." In Canny, 55–78.

Archer, Ian W. "Patronage and clientage in Elizabethan London." In Giry-Deloison, Charles, and Roger Mettam, Eds. *Patronages and clientélismes*. 137–148.

Allen, Don Cameron. *Mysteriously Meant: The Rediscovery of Pagan Symbolism and Allegorical Representation in the Renaissance*. Baltimore: Johns Hopkins UP, 1970.

Allot, Kenneth, Ed. *The Poems of Matthew Arnold.* London: Longmans, 1965.

Armitage, David. "Literature and Empire." In Canny, 99–123.

Ashmolean Museum. *The Earl of Arundel: Patronage and Collecting in the 17th Century*. Exhibition Catalogue November 1985–January 1986.

Ausonius. *Ausonius.* Tr. Hugh G. Evelyn White. Loeb Classical Library Vol. 1. Cambridge: Harvard UP and London: William Heinemann, 1987.

Baker, Hershel, ed. *The Later Renaissance in England: Nondramatic Verse and Prose, 1600–1660.* 1975; rep. Prospect Heights, Illinois: Waveland Press, 1996.

Barkan, Leonard. "Making Pictures Speak: Renaissance Art, Elizabethan Literature, Modern Scholarship. *Renaissance Quarterly* 48 (1995): 326–351.

———."The Beholder's Tale: Ancient Sculpture, Renaissance Narratives. *Representations* 44 (1993): 133–166.

Barnes, Susan. "Van Dyck and George Gage." In Howarth, ed., *Art and Patronage*, 1–11.

Barolsky, Paul. *Giotto's Father and the Family of Vasari's* Lives. University Park: Penn State UP, 1992.

Baxandall, Michael. *Giotto and the Orators: Humanist Observers of Painting in Italy and the Discovery of Pictorial Composition, 1350–1450.* Oxford: Clarendon Press, 1971.

Bedaux, Jan Baptist. "Velázquez's Fable of Arachne (Las Hilanderas): A Continuing Story." *Simiolus* 21 (1992): 296–305.

Boothby, Richard. *A Brief Discovery or Description of the Most Famous Island of Madagascar*. London, 1644.

Bourdieu, Pierre. *Outline of a Theory of Practice.* Tr. Richard Nice. Cambridge: UP, 1977.

Brown, Christopher. *Van Dyck*. Ithaca: Cornell UP 1983.

Burton, Robert. *The Anatony of Melancholy*. Ed. Floyd Dell and Paul Jordan-Smith. New York: Tudor, 1927.

Bylebyl, Jerome J., ed. *William Harvey and His Age:The Professional and Social Context of the Discovery of Circulation*. Baltimore and London: The Johns Hopkins UP, 1979.

Cajori, Florian. *William Oughtred: A Great Seventeenth-Century Mathematician*. Chicago: 1916.

Canny, Nicholas, ed. *The Origins of Empire: British Overseas Enterprise to the Close of the Seventeenth Century.* The Oxford History of thy British Empire. Vol. I. Oxford and New York: Oxford UP, 1998.

Carey, John. *John Donne: Life, Mind, and Art.* New York: Oxford UP, 1981.

Cave, Terence C. *The Cornucopian Text: Problems of Writing in the French Renaissance*. Oxford and New York: Oxford UP, 1979.

Césaire, Aimé. *Une tempête*. Paris: Éditions du Seuil, 1969.

Davenant, Sir William. *The Shorter Poems, and Songs from the Plays and Masques*. Ed. A. M. Gibbs. Oxford: Clarendon P, 1972.

Day, J.F.R. "Primers of Honor: Heraldry, Heraldry Books, and English Renaissance Literature." *Sixteenth-Century Journal* 21 (1990): 93–103.

Debus, Allen G. "Robert Fludd and the Use of Gilbert's *De Magnete* in the Weapon-Salve Controversy." *Journal of the History of Medicine and Allied Sciences* 19 (1964): 389–417.

Delepierre, Octave. *Tableau de la littérature du Centon Chez Les Anciens et chez les Modernes.* 2 Vols. London: 1874.

Demetz, Peter. *Prague in Black and Gold: Scenes from the Life of a European City.* Hill and Wang: New York, 1997.

Deschamps, Hubert. *Histoire de Madagascar.* 3rd ed. Paris: Editions Berger-Levrault, 1965.

Digby, Sir Kenelm. "Observations on…Spencers Faery Queene" (1628?) In *Literary Criticism of 17th-Century England.* Ed. Edward W. Tayler. New York: Knopf, 1967.

———. *A late discourse… touching the cure of wounds by the powder of sympathy.* \4th ed. London, 1664.

Donne, John. *The Poems of John Donne.* Ed. Herbert J.C. Grierson. Vol. I. London: Oxford UP, 1968.

Eco, Umberto.*The Island of the Day Before*. New York: Harcourt, Brace, 1994.

Ellenius, Allan. *De Arte Pingendi.* Uppsala: Almquist and Wiksells, 1960.

Erickson, Robert A. *The Language of the Heart.* Philadelphia: U of Pennsylvania P, 1997.

Evans, Robert C. *Ben Jonson and the Poetics of Patronage.* Lewisburg: Bucknell UP, 1989.

Falco, Raphael. *Conceived Presences: Literary Genealogy in Renaissance England.* Amherst: U of Massachusetts P, 1994.

Fitch-Lytle, Guy and Stephen Orgel, eds. *Patronage in the Renaissance.* Princeton: Princeton UP, 1981.

Ford, Charles. "Portraits and Portraiture in the Literature of Art." *Dutch Crossing* 41 (1990): 110–131.

Fox, Ruth A. *The Tangled Chain: The Structure of Disorder in The Anatomy of Melancholy.* Berkeley: U of California P, 1976.

Frank, Robert G., Jr. *Harvey and the Oxford Physiologists: Scientific Ideas and Social Interaction.* Berkeley and Los Angeles: University of California Press, 1980.

Franklyn, Julian and John Tanne.*An Encyclopaedic Dictionary of Heraldry*. Oxford: Pergamon P, 1969.

French, Roger. *William Harvey's Natural Philosophy*.Cambridge: Cambridge UP, 1994.

Games, Alison. "Sir Thomas Roe and the Integration of the First British

Empire." Paper presented to the Columbia Univ. Seminar on Early American History, New York, 9 February, 1999.

Gay, Peter. *Pleasure Wars*. New York and London: Norton, 1998.

Gilbert, John. *De magnete*. New York: Dover, 1958.

Gillies, John. *Shakespeare and the Geography of Difference*. Cambridge: Cambridge UP, 1994.

Gilman, Ernest B. *Iconoclasm and Poetry in the English Reformation*. Chicago and London: U of Chicago P, 1986.

———. Review of *The Literature of Classical Art*. Ed. Keith Aldrich, Keith, Philipp Fehl, and Raina Fehl. *Renaissance Quarterly* 47 (1994): 551–554.

———. "Sycorax's 'Thing.'" In *Thespis and Solon: Essays on Renaissance Drama and the Law*. Ed. Dennis Kezar. Forthcoming.

Giry-Deloison, Charles, and Roger Mettam, Eds. *Patronages and clientélismes: 1550–1750 (France, Angleterre, Espagne, Italie)*. Lille: Université Charles de Gaulle, 1997.

Grafton, Anthony, et al. *New Worlds, Ancient Texts:The Power of Tradition and the Shock of Discovery*. Cambridge: Harvard UP, 1992.

Greenblatt, Stephen J.*Learning to Curse:Essays in Early Modern Culture*. New York and London: Routledge, 1990.

———. *Shakespearean Negotiations: The Circulation of Social Energy in Renaissance England*. Berkeley and Los Angeles: U. Of California Press, 1988.

Gregory of Nazianzen, Saint. *La Passion du Christ: Tragédie*. Tr. André Tuilier. Paris: 1969.

Griffin, Dustin. *Literary Patronage in England, 1650–1800*. Cambridge: UP, 1996.

Gundersheimer, Werner L."Patronage in the Renaissance: An Exploratory Approach." In Fitch-Lytle, Guy and Stephen Orgel, eds. *Patronage in the Renaissance*. 3–23.

Hagstrum, Jean H. *The Sister Arts: The Tradition of Literary Pictorialism and English Poetry From Dryden to Gray*. Chicago: U of Chicago P, 1958.

Hakluyt Society. *The Voyages of Sir James Lancaster to Brazil and the East Indies 1591–1603*. London, 1940.

Hall, Kim. *Things of Darkness: Economics of Race and Gender in Early Modern England*. Ithaca: Cornell UP, 1995.

Hamond, Richard. *Madagascar: The Richest and Most Fruitful Island in the World*. London, 1643.

Harvey, George. *Henry Clay Frick: The Man*. New York and London: Scribner's, 1928.

Harvey, William. *Disputations touching the Generation of Animals*. Tr. Gweneth Whitteridge. Oxford: Blackwell Scientific Publications, 1981.

———. *On the Motion of the Heart and Blood in Animals*. Tr. Robert Willis. (Translation of *De motu cordis* [1628]) Buffalo: Prometheus Books, 1993.

———. *Works* (1847). Rep. Landmarks of Science Series. Ed. Sir Harold Hartley and Duane H.D. Roller.

Haskell, Francis. *History and its Images: Art and the Interpretation of the Past*. New Haven and London: Yale UP, 1993.

Haskell, Francis and Nicholas Penny. *Taste and the Antique: The Lure of Classical Sculpture 1500–1900.* New Haven and London: Yale UP, 1981.

Haynes, Jonathan. *Humanist as Traveler: George Sandys's Relation of a Journey begun An. Dom. 1610*. London and Toronto: Associated UP, 1986.

Heffernan, James A.W. "Speaking for Pictures: The Rhetoric of Art Criticism." *Word & Image* 15 (1999), 19–33.

Hervey, Mary F.S. *The Life and Correspondence of Thomas Howard Earl of Arundel*. Cambridge: Cambridge UP, 1921.

Heseltine, Nigel. *Madagascar*. New York: Praeger, 1971.

Hill, Christopher. "William Harvey and the Idea of Monarchy." *Past and Present* 27 (1974). Rep. In *The Intellectual Revolution of the Seventeenth Century*. Ed. Charles Webster. London: Routledge, 1974, 160–81.

Hoag, Tara. "Culture and Imperialism: The Fashioning of a Patron, in Two Portraits." Unpublished essay, 1993.

Howarth, David, ed. *Art and Patronage in the Caroline Courts: Essays in Honour of Sir Oliver Millar*. Cambridge: Cambridge UP, 1993.

———. *Images of Rule: Art and Politics in the English Renaissance, 1485–1649*. Berkeley and Los Angeles: U of California P, 1997.

———. "The Politics of Inigo Jones." In Howarth, ed., *Art and Patronage*. Pp. 68–89.

———. *Lord Arundel and his Circle*. New York and London: Yale UP, 1985.

Hynes, D.E.L. *The Arundel Marbles*. Oxford: Oxford UP 1975.

Jonson, Ben. *Seclected Masques*. Ed. Stephen Orgel. New Haven: Yale UP, 1970.

———. *Works*. Ed. C.H. Herford and Percy and Evelyn Simpson. Vol 8: *The Poems*. Oxford: The Clarendon Press, 1947.

Junius, Franciscus. *De Pictura Veterum*. Amsterdam, 1637.

———. *Francisci Junii F.F. De pictura veterum libri tres*. Ed. J.G. Graevius. Rotterdam, 1694.

———.*The Literature of Classical Art*. Ed. Keith Aldrich, Philipp Fehl, and Raina Fehl. 2 vols. Berkeley: U of California P, 1991.

———. *The Painting of the Ancients*. London, 1638 Facs. Gregg International Publishers, 1972.

———. *The Junius Manuscript*. The Anglo-Saxon Poetic Records, I. Ed. G.P. Krapp New York: Columbia UP, 1931.

Keay, John. *The Honourable Company: A History of the East India Company*. New York: Macmillan, 1991.

Knapp, Jeffrey. *An Empire Nowhere: England, America, and Literature from Utopia to the Tempest*. Berkeley and Los Angeles: Univ. Of California Press, 1992.

Lacan, Jacques. *Feiminine Sexuality: Jacques Lacan and the* école freudienne. Ed. Juliet Mitchell and Jacqueline Rose. New York and London: Norton, 1982.

Lee, Rensselaer W. *Ut Pictura Poesis:The Humanistic Theory of Painting*. New York: Norton, 1967.

Lessing, Gotthold Ephraim. *Laocoön: An Essay on the Limits of Poetry and Painting* (1766). Tr. Edward A. McCormick. Indianapolis and New York: Bobbs-Merrill: 1962.

Marshall, David. *The Surprising Effects of Sympathy:Marivaux, Diderot, Rousseau, and Mary Shelley*. Chicago and London: U of Chicago P, 1988.

Mather, Cotton. *The Angel of Bethesda*. Ed. Gordon W. Jones. Barre, MA: American Antiquarian Society and Barre Publishers, 1972.

Marvell, Andrew. *The Poems and Letters of Andrew Marvell*. Ed. H.M. Margoliouth 3rd. Ed. Vol. 1. Oxford: Clarendon Press, 1971.

Michaelis, Adolf. *Ancient Marbles in Great Britain*. Tr. C.A.M. Fennell.

Cambridge: Cambridge UP, 1882.

Millar, Oliver. *Van Dyck in England*. London: National Portrait Gallery, 1982.

Milton Encyclopedia. Ed. William B. Hunter, Jr. Lewisburg: Bucknell UP, 1978.

Milton, John. *Complete Poems and Major Prose*. Ed. Merritt Y. Hughes. New York: Odyssey, 1957.

Mirollo, James V. *Mannerism and Renaissance Poetry: Concept, Mode, Inner Design*. New Haven: Yale UP, 1984.

Mitchell, W.J.T. *Iconology: Image, Text, Ideology*. Chicago and London: U of Chicago P, 1986.

Montrose, Louis A. "The Work of Gender in the Discourse of Discovery." *Representations* 33 (1991): 1–41.

More, Thomas. *Complete Works of St. Thomas More*. Ed. Edward Surtz, S.J. and J.H. Hester. Vol 4 New Haven and London: Yale UP, 1965.

———. *The Correspondence of Sir Thomas More*. Ed. Elizabeth Frances Rogers. Princeton: Princeton UP, 1947.

Mullaney, Steven. "Strange Things, Gross Terms, Curious Customs: The Rehearsal of Cultures in the Late Renaissance." *Representations* 3 (1983): 40–67.

Muller, Jeffrey M. "The Dimension of Time in Anthony van Dyck's Inventions for History Paintings. *Wallraf-Richartz-Jahrbuch* 55 (1994): 127–38.

Nativel, Colette. "Franciscus Junius et le 'De Pictura Veterum.'" *Dix-septieme Siecle* 35 (1983): 7–30. See also her "La Comparison entre la peinture et la poesie dans le De Picture Veterum (1,4) de Franciscus Junius, 1589–1677." *Word and Image* 4 (1988): 323–330.

Nicholson, Marjorie Hope. *The Breaking of the Circle: Studies in the Effect of the "New Science" upon Seventeenth Century Poetry*. Rev. ed. New York: Columbia UP, 1960.

Orgel, Stephen and Roy Strong. *Inigo Jones:The Theatre of the Stuart Court*. 2 vols. London, Berkeley and Los Angeles, 1973.

Oxford Classical Dictionary. 3rd Ed. 1996.

Pagden, Anthony. "The Struggle for Legitamacy and the Image of Empire in the Atlantic to c. 1700." In Canny, 34–54.

Pagel, Walter. *William Harvey's Biological Ideas: Selected Aspects and*

Historical Backgrounds. New York: Hafner, 1967.

Parry, Graham.*The Golden Age restor'd: The Culture of the Stuart Court, 1603–42*. Manchester: Manchester UP, 1981.

Peacham, Henry. *The Complete Gentleman, The Truth of our Times, and The Art of Living in London*. Ed. Virgil B. Heltzel. Ithaca: Cornell UP, 1962.

Peck, Linda Levy, ed. *The Mental World of the Jacobean Court*. Cambridge: Cambridge UP, 1991.

Petersson, R.T. *Sir Kenelm Digby: The Ornament of England, 1603–1665*. Cambridge: Harvard UP, 1956.

Pico della Mirandola. "On the Dignity of Man." In *The Renaissance Philosophy of Man*. Ed. Ernst Cassirer et al. Chicago and London: U of Chicago P, 1948.

Pinto-Correia, Clara. *The Ovary of Eve: Egg and Sperm and Preformation*. Chicago and London: U of Chicago P, 1997.

Rogers, John. *The Matter of Revolution: Science, Poetry, and Politics in the Age of Milton*. Ithaca and London: Cornell UP, 1996.

Salerno, Luigi. "Seventeenth Century English Literature on Painting." *JWCI* 14 (1951): 234–258.

Sanger, Martha Symington. *Henry Clay Frick: An Intimate Portrait*. New York: Abbeville, 1998.

Schnapp, Jeffrey T. "Art/Lit Combines; or, When a Pipe is Only a Pipe." *Profession 1998*. 37–50.

Schreiner, Samuel A., Jr. *Henry Clay Frick: The Gospel of Greed*. New York: St. Martin's, 1995.

Schwartz, Frederic. "'The motions of the countenance': Rembrandt's Early Portraits and the Tronie." *RES* 17–18 (1989): 89–116.

Schwartz, Regina. "Real Hunger: Milton and Reformaton Poetics." Lecture. CUNY Graduate Center, November, 1998.

Shakespeare, William. *The Tempest*. Ed. Frank Kermode. The Arden Edition of the Works of William Shakespeare. Sixth edition. Cambridge, MA.: Harvard UP, 1958.

———. *The Tempest*. Ed. Stephen Orgel. The Oxford Shakespeare. Oxford: Clarendon Press, 1987 [all citations from this edition].

Seelig, Sharon Cadmon. *Generating Texts: The Progeny of Seventeenth-Century Prose*. Charlottesville: UP of Virginia, 1996.

Selden, John. *Marmora Arundeliana*. London, 1628.

———. *Titles of Honour.* 2nd. Ed. London, 1631.

Sibree, James. *The Great African Island: Chapters on Madagascar.* London, 1880.

Sidney, Philip. *Sir Philip Sidney: A Critical Edition of the Major Works.* Ed. Katherine Duncan- Jones. Oxford and New York: Oxford UP, 1989.

Smuts, Malcolm. "Cultural Diversity and Cultural Change at the Court of James I." In Peck, ed., *Mental World.* 99–112.

———. "The Political Failure of Stuart Cultural Patronage." In Fitch-Lytle, Guy and Stephen Orgel, eds. *Patronage in the Renaissance.* 165–187.

Sobel, Dava. *Longitude: The True Story of a Lone Genius Who Solved the Greatest Scientific Problem of His Time.* New York: Penguin, 1995.

Springell, Francis C. *Connoisseur and Diplomat: The Earl of Arundel's Embassy to Germany in 1636.* London: 1963.

Stewart, Susan. *On Longing: Narratives of the Miniature, the Gigantic, the Souvenir, the Collection.* Durham and London: Duke UP, 1993.

Sumner, Ann, ed. *Death, Passion and Politics: Van Dyck's Portraits of Venetia Stanley and George Digby.* London: Dulwich Picture Gallery, 1995.

Taplin, Gardner B. *The Life of Elizabeth Barrett Browning.* London: John Murray, nd.

Tenison, Thomas. *Baconiana.* London: 1679.

Trevor-Roper, Hugh. *Princes and Artists:Patronage and Ideology at Four Hapsburg Courts, 1517–1633.* New York: Harper & Row, 1976.

Usher, M.D. *Homeric Stichings: The Homeric Centos of the Empress Eudocia.* Lanham, MD and New York: Rowman & Littlefield, 1998.

Van Dyck, Anthony. *Van Dyck: Paintings.* Ed. Arthur K. Wheelock, Jr., et al. Washington: National Gallery of Art, 1990

Warnke, Martin. "Kunst vor ihrer Geschichte: zum kunsthistoriographischen Verfahren des Franciscus Junius." *Wolfenebütteler Forschungen* 48 (1991): 135–43.

Webster, Charles. "William Harvey and the Crisis of Medicine in Jacobean England." In Bylebyl, 1–27.

Wendorf, Richard. The Elements of Life: Biography and Portrait Paint-

ing in Stuart and Georgian England. Oxford: Clarendon Press, 1990.

Whitteridge, Gweneth. *William Harvey and the Circulation of the Blood.* London: Macdonald, 1971.

Winckelmann, Johann Joachim. *Geschichte der Kunst des Alterthums,* 1764.

Wood, Christopher S. "'Curious pictures' and the Art of Description." *Word & Image* 11 (1995): 332–52.

Woolf, D.R. "Erudition and the Idea of History in Renaissance England." *Renaissance Quarterly* 40 (1987): 11–48.

Ziff, Jerrold. "Turner, the Ancients, and the Dignity of Art." *Turner Studies* 3 (1984): 45–59.

Index

Literature and the Visual Arts
New Foundations

Ernest B. Gilman
General Editor

Offering works of scholarship and criticism on the interrelationship of literature and the visual arts, this series reflects the rich diversity of subjects and approaches in this developing field. Our authors contribute to an expert's understanding of the topic. At the same time, they speak to readers, lay and professional, with a more general interest in the area. Ideally—and this is the thrust of the phrase "New Foundations" in our series title—works published under the imprint focus on the ways their particular concern leads us to rethink the basic questions of comparative study between the arts, challenging the reader volume by volume continually to remap the grounds, historical and theoretical, on which such inquiry can take place at all.

For additional information about this series or for the submission of manuscripts, please contact:

Acquisitions Department
Peter Lang Publishing
275 Seventh Avenue, 28th floor
New York, New York 10001

To order other books in this series, please contact our Customer Service Department:

(800) 770-LANG (within the U.S.)
(212) 647-7706 (outside the U.S.)
(212) 647-7707 FAX

Or browse online by series at:

www.peterlangusa.com